GW00786397

# Introduction to
# Autodesk Revit 5.0

## Daniel John Stine

ISBN: 1-58503-123-2

**PUBLICATIONS**

**Schroff Development Corporation**

**www.schroff.com**
www.schroff-europe.com

# *Forward*

**To The Student:**
The intent of this book is to provide the student with a well-rounded knowledge of tools and techniques for use in both school and industry.

It is strongly recommended that this book is completed in lesson order. Many exercises utilize drawings created in previous lessons.

**To the Instructor:**
This book was designed for the architectural student using Autodesk Revit 5.0. Throughout the book the student develops a three story office building. The drawings start with the floor plans and develop all the way to photo-realistic renderings like the one on the cover of this book.

Throughout the book many Revit tools and techniques are covered while creating the office building model. Also, in a way that is applicable to the current exercise, general building codes and industry standard conventions are covered.

An Instructor's resource guide is available with this book. It contains:
- Answers to the questions at the end of each chapter
- Outline of tools & topics to be covered in each lessons lecture
- Suggestions for additional student work  (for each lesson)

**About the Author:**
Dan Stine has eleven years experience in the architectural field. He currently works at Stanius Johnson Architects in Duluth Minnesota as a Drafter/Cad Manager. Dan has worked in three firm's total. While at these firms, Dan has participated in collaborative projects with several other firms on various projects (including Cesar Pelli, Weber Music Hall – University of Minnesota - Duluth). All of these firms have their own CAD standards and customization. This has given Dan a fairly well rounded knowledge of optimizing and implementing CAD standards and customization. More specifically, Dan has experience programming (general/AutoCAD), 3D modeling, customizing and optimally configuring AutoCAD, Web page design (general/project collaboration), and general maintenance of Window 2000 server. Dan has taught CAD classes for the last four years at Lake Superior College, for the Architectural Technology program; including an Advanced AutoCAD for Architecture class (a class based on Dan's book; *"Essentials for Architecture using Architectural Desktop R3.3"* published by Schroff Development Corporation).

You can contact Dan with comments or suggestions at **dan.stine@charter.net**
*Please do not email with Revit questions unless they relate to a problem with this book.*

**Thanks:**
I could not have done this with out the support from my family; Cheri, Kayla & Carter. They had to bear with me a few nights while daddy had to work on the book. I love you guys!

I also want to thank Autodesk for providing the Revit software.

Many thanks go out to Stephen Schroff and Schroff Development Corporation for making this book possible!

# Table of Contents

# Lesson 1
# Getting Started with Autodesk Revit 5.0::

This chapter will introduce you to Autodesk Revit 5.0. We will cover the User Interface. You will also learn how to open and exit a project and adjust the view of the drawing on the screen. It is recommended that the student spend an ample amount of time learning this material, as it will greatly enhance your ability to progress smoothly through subsequent chapters.

## Exercise 1-1:
## What is Autodesk Revit 5.0?

## What is Autodesk Revit 5.0 used for?

Autodesk Revit 5.0 is the world's first fully parametric architectural design software. This revolutionary software, for the first time, truly takes computer aided design beyond simply being a high tech pencil. Autodesk Revit 5.0 is a product of Autodesk, makers of AutoCAD, Architectural Desktop and 3D Studio Max. The Autodesk company web site claims more than 4 million users in 160 countries. Autodesk's 3,600 employees create products available in 20 languages.

## What is a parametric building modeler?

Revit is a relatively new program designed from the ground up using state-of-the-art technology. The term parametric describes a process by which an object is modified in one view and automatically updated in all other views and schedules. For example if you move a door in an interior elevation view, the floor plan will automatically update. Or, if you delete a door, it will be deleted from all other views and schedules. You can even delete a door from the door schedule and the drawing will instantly be revised to reflect the change.

A major goal of Revit is to eliminate much of the repetitive and mundane tasks traditionally associated with CAD programs to allow more time for design and visualization.

The best way to understand how a parametric model works is to describe the Revit project file. A single Revit file contains your entire building project. Even though you mostly draw in 2D view, you are actually drawing in 3D. In fact, the entire building project is a 3D model. From this 3D model you can generate elevations, sections and perspective views. Therefore, when you delete a door in an elevation view you are actually deleting the door from the 3D model from which all 2D views are generated.

## Why use Revit 5.0?

Many people ask the question, why use Revit versus other programs? The answer can certainly vary depending on the situation and particular needs of an individual/organization.

Generally speaking, this is why most companies use Revit:
- Many designers and drafters are using Revit to streamline repetitive drafting tasks and focus more on designing and detailing a project.
- Revit is a very progressive program and offers many feature for designing buildings. Revit is a subscription-based program and provides incremental upgrades/patches on a regular basis.
- Revit was designed specifically for architecture and includes features like:
  - Accurender's Photo-realistic renderer
  - RS Means CostWorks estimating module
  - Pantone digital color

With the recent acquisition of Revit by Autodesk and the statement on their web site that this is the path they will develop long-term, Revit will quickly become the industry standard in architectural modeling. With a solid company like Autodesk behind Revit, a prospective user can be fairly certain that the investment in time and resources will ultimately pay off.

## The future is limitless.

Once this technology is embraced as the industry standard, and maybe sooner, we can expect some amazing advancements in the program. For example, with the building being a 3D model, we will see building code analyzers with plug-in modules for state and local codes, similar to tax programs like TurboTax. We might also see structural, mechanical & electrical engineers designing in the same model as the architects (maybe over a high speed internet connection for remote consultants). This would eliminate conflicts found in many drawings today.

## Exercise 1-2:
## Overview of the Revit User Interface

Revit is a powerful and sophisticated program. Because of its powerful feature set it has a measurable learning curve, though its intuitive design makes it easier to learn than other CAD programs. However, like anything, when broken down into smaller pieces, we can easily learn to harness the power of Revit. That is the goal of this book.

This section will walk through the different sections of the User Interface (UI). Like any program, understanding the user interface is the key to using the programs features.

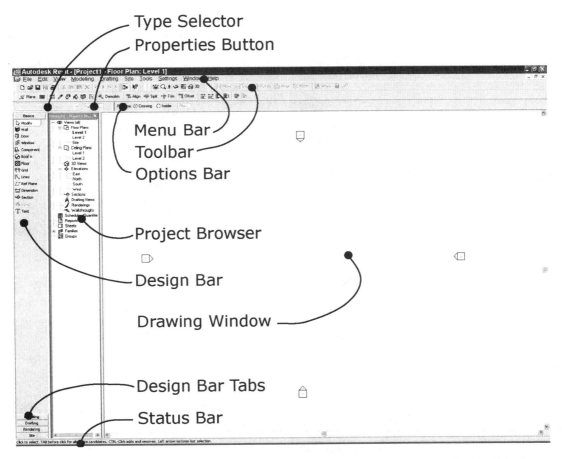

**Figure 1-1** Revit User Interface

## The Revit User Interface:

Menu bar:
Like all Windows programs, Revit has a series of pull-down menus across the top of the screen. Click on each of the menus to explore their contents. Many of these commands are graphically represented by Toolbars and the Design Bar.

Toolbar - Standard:
The standard toolbar contains commands found in most Windows programs. Some examples are: Open, Save, Cut, Copy, Paste, and Print.

Toolbar - View:
This toolbar allows you to adjust the current drawing windows view. You can Zoom in & out, Pan and switch to 3D Views.

Toolbar - Edit:
Contains commands that modify objects in the drawings, i.e., Move, Mirror, Array, Group, Rotate.

Toolbar - Tools:
Contains common commands that modify objects in the drawings, i.e., Trim, Split, Offset, Tape Measure.

Worksets - Toolbar:
This toolbar allows you to manage and work with Worksets. Worksets allow multiple users to work on the same project (i.e. same project file).

Options Bar:
This "toolbar" dynamically changes to show options that compliment the current operation.

Project Browser:
The project browser shows all the views, families and groups available in the current project. A view is a floor plan, elevation or ceiling plan of the model.

Design Bar:
This area is like an enhanced Menu Bar. Each tab (see Design Bar Tabs next) displays commands related to the tab title. This area also dynamically changes to show options related to the current operation.

Design Bar Tabs:    The Design Bar Tabs are groupings of commands in the Design Bar area. The current tab is the tab located at the bottom of the top group of tabs. Notice when you select a Design Bar Tab (e.g. Structural) that the tabs above it also slide to the top. Think of it like drawers of design tools.
*TIP: Right-click on a tab to see a pop-up menu that allows you to turn on & off various tab groups.*

Status Bar:    This area will display information about the current command or list information about a selected object.

Drawing Window:    This is where you design your project and generate views and schedules.

Type Selector:    The Type Selector lists the available families for the current operation. e.g. When inserting door you can select different door styles and sizes; when inserting walls you can select various wall types to draw.

Properties Button:    This button allows you to view the various properties of the selected components. Many of the properties are editable here as well.


This concludes our brief overview of the Revit user interface. Many of these tools and operations will be covered in more detail throughout the book.

## Exercise 1-3:
## Open, Save & Close an existing Project

Open **Autodesk Revit 5.0**
*Start → All Programs → Autodesk Revit 5.0*
(Figure 1-2 – *Note:* Windows XP Start menu shown).

Or double-click the Revit icon from your desktop.

Autodesk
Revit 5.0

This may vary slightly on your computer; see your instructor or system administrator if you need help.

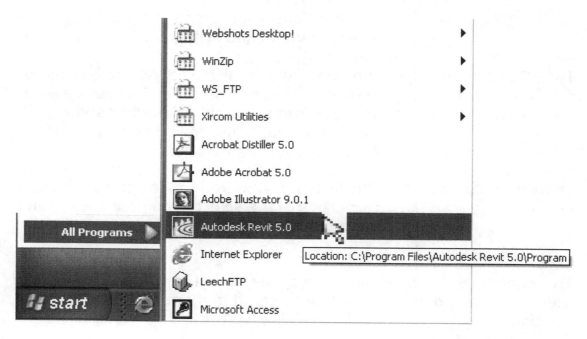

**Figure 1-2** Starting Revit

## Open an existing Revit project:

By default, Revit will open a new (empty) project. So, the first thing we will do is close this project.

1.   Select **File → Close** from the menu bar.

Next you will open an existing Revit project file. You will select a sample file that was installed with the Revit program.

2. Select **File → Open** from the menu bar.

3. Browse to the following folder: **C:\Program Files\Autodesk Revit 5.0\Training\Imperial**.

4. Select the file named **Cohouse.rvt** and click **Open**.

The Cohouse file is now open and the last saved view is displayed in the Drawing Window.

The Window pull-down menu on the menu bar lists the projects and views currently open on your computer.

5. Click **Window** from the menu bar (Figure 1-3).

Notice that the Cohouse project file is listed. Next to the project name is the name of a view (e.g. floor plan, elevation) open on your computer.

**Figure 1-3** Window menu

Additional views will be added to the list as you open them. Each view has the project name as a prefix. The current view (i.e. the view you are working in) has a check mark next to it. You can quickly toggle between opened views from this menu.

## Open another existing Revit project:

Revit also lets you open more than one project at a time.

6. Click **File → Open** from the menu bar.

7. Browse to the following folder: **C:\Program Files\Autodesk Revit 5.0\Training\Imperial**.

8. Select the file named **Cost Model.rvt** and click **Open**.

9. Click **Window** from the menu bar (Figure 1-4).

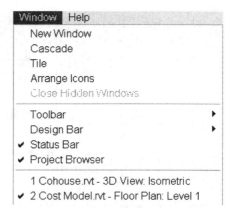

**Figure 1-4** Window menu

Notice that the Cost Model project is now listed along with a view (*Floor Plan: Level 1 in this example*).

Try toggling between projects by clicking on *Cohouse.rvt – 3D View: Isometric*.

## Close a Revit project:

10. Select **File → Close** from the menu bar.

This will close the current project/view. If more than one view is open for a project, only the current view will close. The project and the other opened views will not close.

11. Repeat step 10 to close the other project file.

If you have not saved your view yet, you will be prompted to do so before Revit closes the view. **Do not save at this time**.

## Saving a Revit project:

**At this time we will not actually save a project.**

To save a Project view, simply select **File → Save** from the file menu. You can also click the save icon from the Standard Toolbar.

You should get in the habit of saving often to avoid loosing work due to a power outage or program crash.

## Closing the Revit program:

Finally, from the File pull-down menu select Exit. This will close any open projects/view and shut Revit down. Again you will be prompted to save (if needed) before Revit closes the view. Do not save at this time.

You can also click the red X in the upper right corner of the Revit window. (*The icon is red in Window XP only.*)

## Exercise 1-4:
## Creating a new Project

**Open Autodesk Revit 5.0**

## Creating a new project file:

The steps required to set up a new Revit building model project file are very simple. As mentioned earlier, simply opening the Revit program starts you in a new unnamed project file.

To manually create a new project (maybe you just finished working on a previous assignment and want to start the next one):

1.  Select **File → New → Project...** from the file menu bar
    Or select the New icon from the Standard Toolbar.

    If you select the *New* icon, a new project is quickly setup using the default template.

    If you select *File → New → Project...* from the menu bar, you will get the **New Project** dialog box (Figure 1-5).

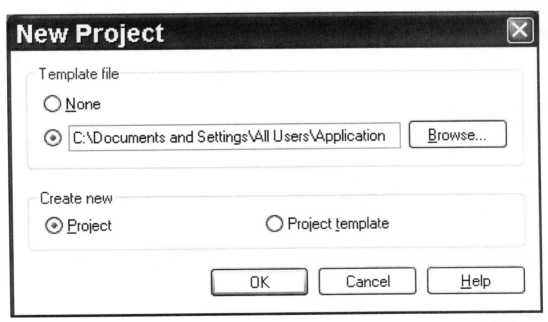

**Figure 1-5** New Project dialog box

The New Project dialog box lets you specify the template file you want to use, or not use a template at all. You can also specify whether you want to create a new project or template file.

2.  Leave the **default.Rte** *Template file* selected (you need to click in the text box and arrow key to the right to see the template file name), and *Create new* set to **Project** (Figure 1-5).

3.  You now have a new "unnamed" project file.

To name an unnamed project file you simply save. The first time an unnamed project file is saved you will be prompted to specify the name and location for the project file.

4.  Select **File → Save** from the menu bar.

5.  Specify a **name** and **location** for your new project file.
    *Your instructor may specify a location or folder for your files in this class.*

## What is a template file?

A template file allows you to start your project with certain settings preset the way you like or need them.

For example, you can have the units set to Imperial or Metric. You can have the door, window and wall families you use most loaded and eliminate others less often used. You can have your companies title block preloaded.

A custom template is a must for design firms using Revit and will prove useful to the student as he or she becomes more proficient with the program.

---

**Be Aware:**
It will be assumed from this point forward that the reader understands how to create, open and save project files. Please refer back to this section as needed. If you still need further assistance ask you instructor for help.

## Exercise 1-5:
## Using Zoom & Pan to view your drawings

Learning to Pan and Zoom in and out of a drawing is essential to accurate and efficient drafting and visualization. We will review these commands now so you are ready to use them with the first design exercise.

Open **Autodesk Revit 5.0**.

We will select a sample file that was installed with the Revit program.

1. Select **File** → **Open** from the menu bar.

2. Browse to the following folder: **C:\Program Files\Autodesk Revit 5.0\Training\Imperial**.

3. Select the file named **Drawing_exercise.rvt** and click **Open** (Figure 1-6).

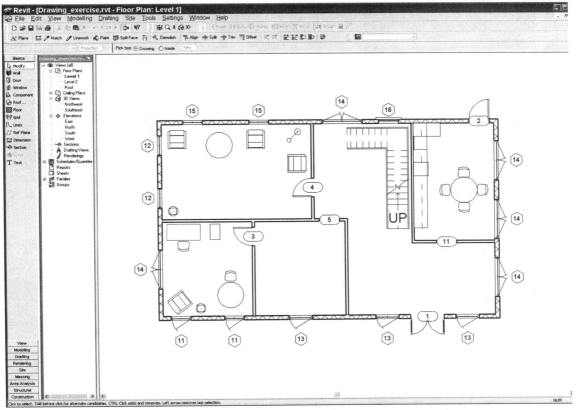

**Figure 1-6** Drawing_exercise.rvt project

If the default view that is loaded is not **Floor Plan: Level 1**, double-click on **Level 1** under **Floor Plans** in the *project browser*. Level 1 will be bold.

## Using Zoom and Pan tools:

You can access the zoom tools from the **View Toolbar,** or the *View* pull-down menu and the *scroll wheel* on your mouse.

View Toolbar commands (from left to right)
- Dynamically modify view
- Zoom In *(includes drop-down arrow for additional zoom tools)*
- Hide/Isoloate *(to be covered in a later lesson)*
- Thin Lines *(to be covered in a later lesson)*
- Default 3D view

**Zoom In**

1. Select the zoom icon by clicking directly on the magnifying glass (not the down arrow).

2. Drag a window over your plan view (Figure 1-7).

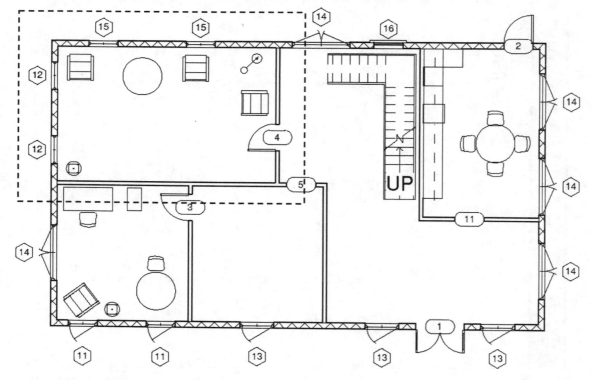

**Figure 1-7** Zoom In window

You should now be zoomed in to the specified area (Figure 1-8).

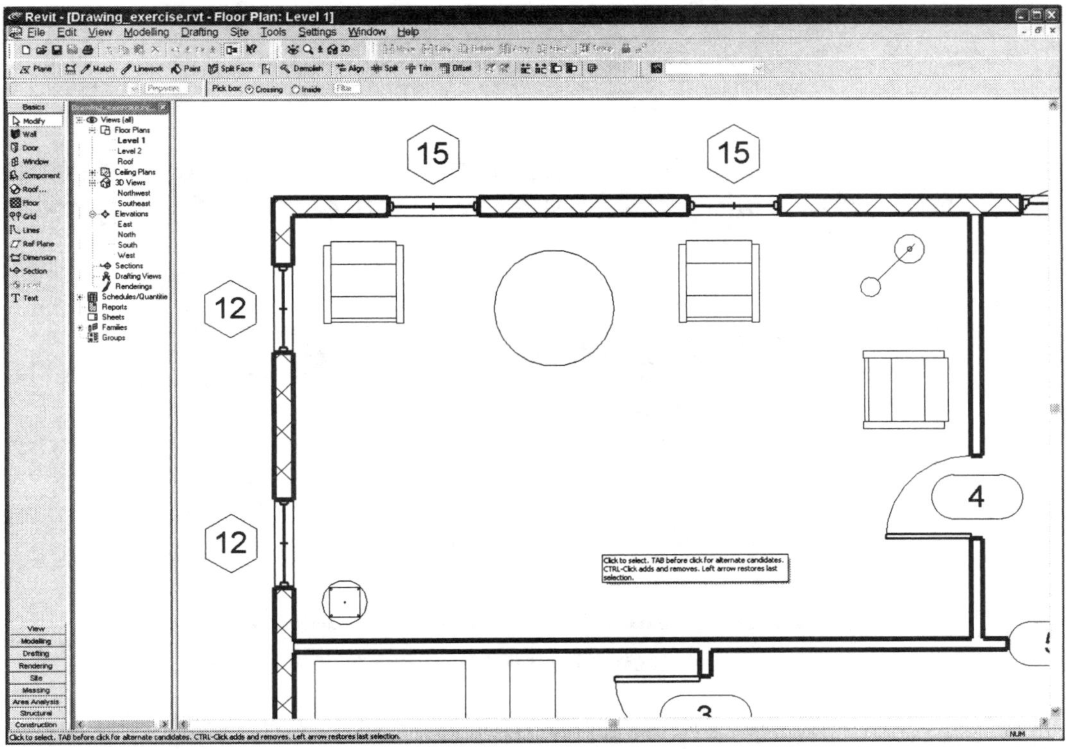

**Figure 1-8** Zoom In results

## Zoom Out

3. Click the down-arrow next to the zoom icon (Figure 1-9). Select **Previous Scroll/Zoom**.

You should now be back where you started.

Take a minute and try the other zoom tools to see how they work. When finished, click **Zoom All to Fit** before moving on.

Zoom In Region
Zoom Out (2x)
Zoom To Fit
Zoom All to Fit

Previous Scroll/Zoom
Next Scroll/Zoom

**Figure 1-9** Zoom Icon drop-down

## Dynamically Modify View

The *Dynamically Modify View* tool allows you to perform a real-time zoom and pan in your drawing view.

1.  Click the **Dynamically Modify View** icon; you should see the Dynamic View dialog box at the lower left corner of your screen (Figure 1-10).

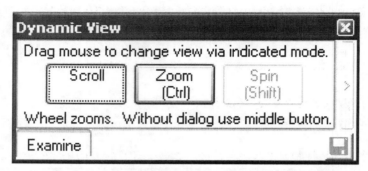

**Figure 1-10** Dynamic View dialog box

2.  You are automatically in Scroll mode. Drag your mouse (holding left button) around the screen in the drawing window to scroll (*also called* panning) the view of your drawing in the window.

> **Be Aware:**
> You are not moving the drawing. You are just changing what part of the drawing you see in the drawing window.

Next we will try the real-time zoom. You can click the Zoom button in the Dynamic View dialog (Figure 1-10) or you can simply hold down the Control (Ctrl) Key on the keyboard to toggle into Zoom mode. Using the Ctrl key is a quick way to switch back and forth between Pan & Zoom.

3.  Hold down the Ctrl key and drag your mouse up or down (vertically) in the drawing window.

The Spin option is only available in 3D views. We will try this shortly.

## Default 3D View

Clicking on the Default 3D View icon loads a 3D View in another drawing window. This allows you to quickly switch between 2D views and 3D views.

1. Click on the **Default 3D View** icon.

2. Click on the **Window** pull-down menu and notice the 3D view and the Floor Plan view are both listed at the bottom. *Remember you can toggle between views here.*

3. Click the **Esc** key to close the Window menu.

4. Click the **Dynamically Modify View** icon.  *Notice the Spin button is now active (Figure 1-11).*

5. Click on the **Spin button** (Figure 1-11) *or hold down the Shift key*, then drag the mouse in any direction (horiz. or vert.) in the 3D view. **Close** the project without saving.

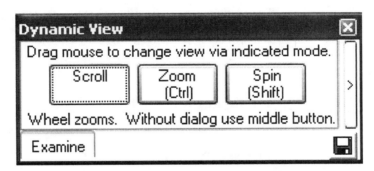

**Figure 1-11** Dynamic View dialog

## Using the Scroll wheel on the mouse

The scroll wheel on the mouse is one of the best improvements to the computer in recent years. In Revit you can Pan and Zoom without even clicking a zoom icon. You simply **scroll the wheel to zoom** and **hold the wheel button down to pan**. This can be done while in another command (e.g. while drawing walls). Another nice feature is that the drawing zooms into the area near your cursor, rather than zooming only at the center of the drawing window like the Dynamic View tool does.

## Self-Exam:

The following questions can be used as a way to check your knowledge of this lesson. The answers can be found on the last page of this section.

1.  The View Toolbar allows you to save your project file. (T/F)

2.  You can zoom in and out using the wheel on a wheel mouse. (T/F)

3.  Revit is parametric architectural design software. (T/F)

4.  A _____ file allows you to start your project with certain setting preset the way you like or need them.

5.  In the Revit user interface, projects are viewed in the _____ window.


## Review Questions:

The following questions may be assigned by your instructor as a way to assess your knowledge of this section. Your instructor has the answers to the review questions.

1.  The Options Toolbar dynamically changes to show options at compliment the current operation. (T/F)

2.  Revit is strictly a 2D drafting program. (T/F)

3.  The Projects/Views listed at the bottom of the Window pull-down menu allow you to see which Projects/Views are currently open. (T/F)

4.  When you use the scroll tool you are actually moving the drawing, not just changing what part of the drawing you can see on the screen. (T/F)

5.  Revit was not originally created for architecture. (T/F)

6.  The icon with the floppy disk icon ( ) allows you to _____ a project file.

7.  Clicking on the _____ next to the Zoom In icon will list additional zoom tools not currently shown in the view toolbar.

8.  When using the Dynamically Modify View tool, the Spin button is inactive unless you are in a _____ view.

# Lesson 2
# Lake Cabin: FLOOR PLAN::

In this lesson you will get a down and dirty overview of the functionality of Revit. We will cover the very basics of creating the primary components of a floor plan: Walls, Doors, Windows, Roof, Annotation & Dimensioning. Future lesions will cover these features in more detail while learning other editing tools and such along the way.

## Exercise 2-1:
### Walls

In this exercise we will draw the walls, starting with the exterior.

Tracing Paper Sketch of Lake Cabin Plan:

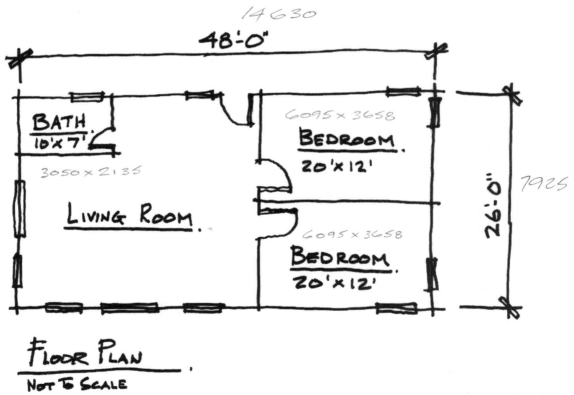

**Figure 2-1** Lake Cabin Sketch

## Exterior Walls:

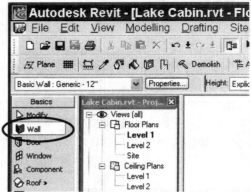

**Figure 2-2** Wall tool

1.  Start a new project named **Lake Cabin**. *See lesson 1 on creating a new project.*

2.  Click on the **Wall** tool under the *Basics* tab in the **Design Bar** (Figure 2-2).

Notice that the Options Bar has changed to show options related to walls. Next we will modify those settings.

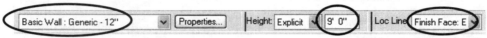

**Figure 2-3** Options Bar

3.  Modify the **options bar** to the following (Figure 2-3):
    a. *Type Selector*: Click the down-arrow and select **Basic: Generic – 12"**.
    b. *Height*: Change the height from 20'-0" to **9'-0"**.
    c. *Loc Line*: Set this to **Finish Face : Exterior**.

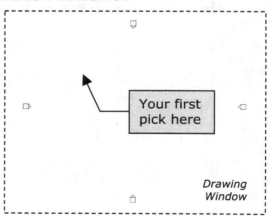

We are now ready to draw the exterior walls.

4.  In the Drawing Window, click in the upper left corner.

5.  Start moving the mouse to the right. Click when the wall is **48'-0"** long.

Notice as you move the mouse Revit dynamically displays a length and an angle. If you want a horizontal line you move the mouse straight across the screen. A dashed line & a tool tip will appear when the line is snapped to the horizontal (Figure 2-4).

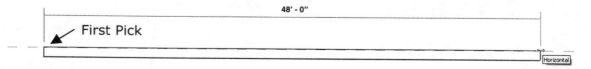

**Figure 2-4** First wall segment

If your mouse moved a little when you clicked and the wall is not exactly 48'-0", simply click on the dimension and type 48' and press enter.

You are now ready to pick the first point of your second line.

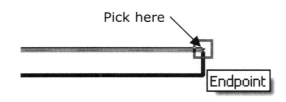

6.  Click the right end of the first line, making sure you snap to the outside corner of your building. (Figure 2-5)

**Figure 2-5** Second wall start point

You may need to zoom in to pick the correct point; see Lesson 1 for zooming.

7.  Start moving your mouse straight down (south), while the dashed line & tool tip appear (indicating a vertical line), type **26'** and press enter.

Typing the length allows you to accurately input a length with out having to spend a lot of time setting the mouse in just the right position. However, you can still adjust the dimension after the line is drawn.

8.  Draw the other two exterior walls.

## Interior Walls:

9.  With the Wall tool selected, modify the **options bar** to the following:
    a. *Type Selector*: Click the down-arrow and select **Basic: Generic – 5"**.
    b. *Loc Line*: Set this to **Core Centerline**.

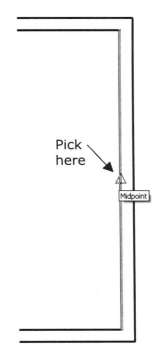

10. Draw wall between bedrooms. Snap to the midpoint of the east wall. (Figure 2-6)

11. While moving the mouse to the west (left) and snapped to the horizontal plane, type **20'2 1/2**.

    Note: Type the length as shown; you don't need a dash or the inch symbol as they are assumed here. You do need a space before the fraction.

**Figure 2-6** Interior wall start point

6095 + 70
= 6165

12. Draw the vertical wall to close off the bedrooms. Revit allows you to do this with one wall segment by selecting you points in a particular way. See **Figure 2-7** for a graphical description of this process. (Figure 2-7)

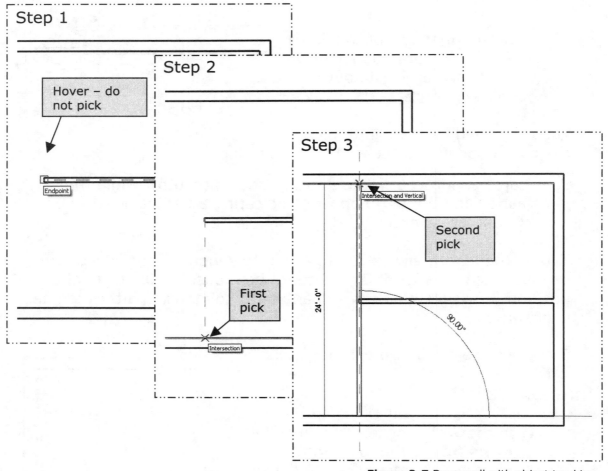

**Figure 2-7** Draw wall with object tracking

13. Draw the two interior walls for the bathroom to complete the interior walls. (Figure 2-1)

14. **Save** your project.

TIP: You can use the **Tape Measure** tool to list the dimension between two points. This is helpful when you want to verify the clear dimension between walls and Revit is displaying a distance that is to the centerline of a wall. Simply click the icon and snap to two points and Revit will temporarily display the distance.

## Exercise 2-2:
## Doors

In this exercise you will add doors to your cabin floor plan.

1. Open **Lake Cabin.rvt** created in exercise 2-1.

## Placing doors:

2. Click on the **Door** tool under the *Basics* tab in the **Design Bar**. (Figure 2-8)

Notice that the *Options Bar* has changed to show options related to Doors. Next we will modify those settings.

The *Type Selector* indicates the door style, width & height. Clicking the down arrow to the right lists all the doors loaded into the current project.

**Figure 2-8** Door tool

The default template project that we started from has several sizes for a single flush door. Notice that the there are two standard heights in the list. The 80" (6'-8") doors are the standard residential height and the 84" (7'-0") doors are the standard commercial door height.

3. Change the type selector to **Sgl Flush: 36" x 80"**.

4. Move your cursor over a wall and position the door as shown in **Figure 2-10**. Notice that the swing of the door changes depending on what side of the wall your cursor is. (Figure 2-10)

5. Click to place the door. Revit automatically trims the wall.

6. While the door is still selected, click on the *change swing (control arrows)* symbol to make the door swing against the wall.

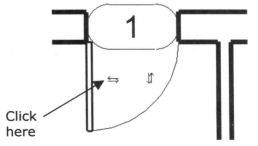

Click here

**Figure 2-9** Changing door swing

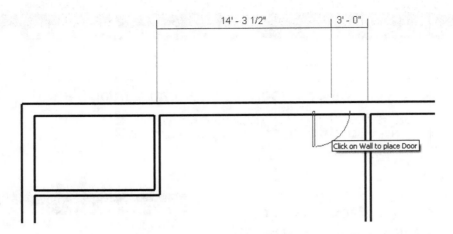

**Figure 2-10** Dynamic graphical info during door insertion

Revit allows you to continue inserting doors until you select a different tool from the toolbar or design bar.

7.  Insert the doors into the bedrooms as shown in **Figure 2-1**. The exact position is not important in this exercise.

8.  Change the *Type Selector* to **Sgl Flush: 30" x 80"**.

9.  Insert a door into the bathroom.

## Deleting doors:

Next you will learn how to delete a door when needed. This process will work for most objects (i.e., walls, windows, text, etc.) in Revit.

10. Insert a door between the two bedrooms.

11. Click on the **Modify** tool on the *Design Bar*. (Figure 2-11)
    Tip: Any time you press the Esc key Revit reverts to Modify.

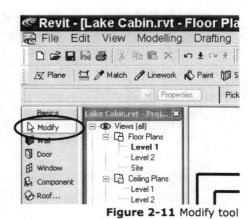

12. Click on the door you just inserted and press the **Delete key** on your keyboard.

13. **Save** your project.

**Figure 2-11** Modify tool

## Exercise 2-3:
## Windows

In this exercise you will add windows to your cabin floor plan.

1.  Open **Lake Cabin.rvt** created in exercise 2-2.

### Placing Windows:

2.  Click on the **Window** tool under the *Basics* tab on the **Design Bar**. (Figure 2-8)

Notice that the Options Bar has changed to show options related to Windows. Next we will modify those settings.

The *Type Selector* indicates the Window style, width & height. Clicking the down arrow to the right lists all the windows loaded in the current project.

**Figure 2-12** Window tool

3.  Change the type selector to **Fixed: 36" x 72"**.

4.  Move your cursor over a wall and place two windows as shown in **Figure 2-13**. Notice that the position of the window changes depending on what side of the wall your cursor is. (Figure 2-13)

5.  Change the type selector to **Fixed: 24" x 72"**.

6.  Place the other 4 windows in the living room area as shown in **Figure 2-1**. Again, in this exercise we are not concerned with the exact placement of the windows.

7.  Change the type selector to **Fixed: 24" x 48"**.

8.  Place the remaining 5 windows (two in each bedroom & one in the bath room) shown in **Figure 2-1**.

9.  **Save** your project.

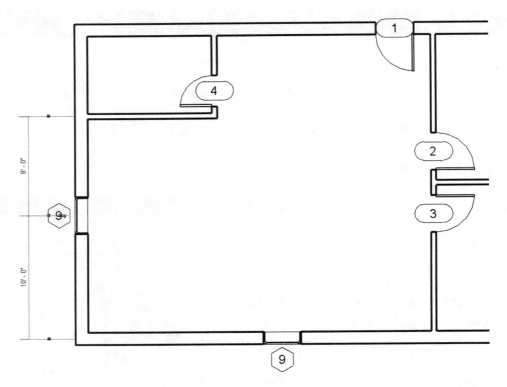

**Figure 2-13** Two large windows

## Snap Symbols:

By now you should be well aware of the snaps that Revit suggests as you move your cursor about the drawing window.

If you hold your cursor still for a moment while a snap symbol is displayed, a tool tip will appear on the screen. However, when you become familiar with the snap symbols you can pick sooner. (Figure 2-14)

The TAB key cycles through the available snaps near your cursor.

The keyboard shortcut turns off the other snaps for one pick. For example, if you type SE on the keyboard while in the Wall command, Revit will only look for an endpoint for the next pick.

Finally, typing SO (snaps off) turns all snaps off for one pick.

| Symbol | Position | Keyboard Shortcut |
|--------|----------|-------------------|
| ✕ | Intersection | SI |
| □ | Endpoint | SE |
| △ | Midpoint | SM |
| ○ | Center | SC |
| ✕ | Nearest | SN |
| ⌐ | Perpendicular | SP |
| ⌀ | Tangent | ST |

**Figure 2-14** Snap Reference Chart

# Exercise 2-4:
## Roof

You will now add a simple roof to your lake cabin.

1. Open **Lake Cabin.rvt** created in exercise 2-3.

## Sketching a roof:

2. Click on the **Roof** tool under the *Basics* tab in the **Design Bar**; a fly-out menu will appear. (Figure 2-15)

The fly-out prompts you for the method you want to use to create the roof.

3. Click **Roof by footprint**.

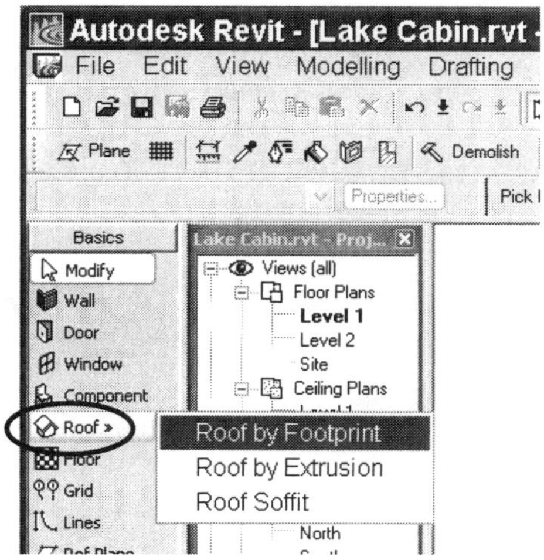

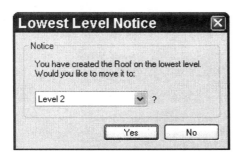

**Figure 2-15** Roof tool

*Roof is on the Lowest Level warning*
Revit notices that you are on level 1 and asks you if you want to switch to another level. In our case we want to switch to level 2. (Figure 2-16)

**Figure 2-16** Roof is on the Lowest Level prompt

4. Make sure **Level 2** is selected and click **Yes**.

You are now on level 2 and ready to sketch the roof footprint. Notice the Level 1 walls are light grey because they are on the level below the current level.

Also notice the *Design Bar* has temporarily been replaced with Sketch options relative to the roof (Figure 2-17), as with the Options Bar (2-18).

**Figure 2-18**
Roof sketch options

**Figure 2-17**
Roof sketch tools

5.  Pick each of the exterior walls to specify the roof footprint. *Be sure to pick the exterior side of the wall.*

6.  Click **Finish Roof** on the *Design Bar*.

You should be back on Level 1. You can see this in the project browser (i.e., Level 1 is bold).

7.  To see the roof click the **Default 3D View** icon.  (Figure 2-19)

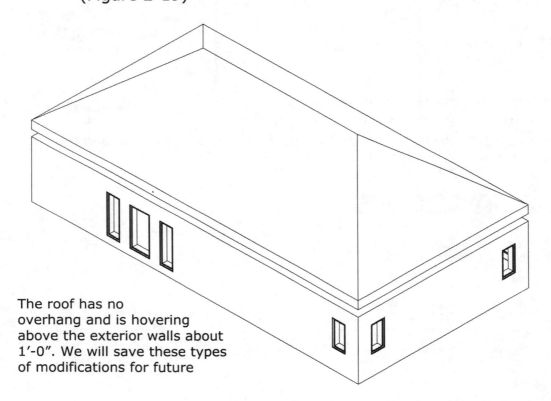

The roof has no overhang and is hovering above the exterior walls about 1'-0". We will save these types of modifications for future

**Figure 2-19** Default 3D View

8.  Click the **X** in the upper right corner of the *Drawing Window* to close the current view (3D). This will close the 3D view but not the project or the Level 1 view.

9.  **Save** your project.

## Exercise 2-5:
## Annotation & Dimensions

Adding text is very simply in Revit. In this exercise we will add labels to each room in our lake cabin plan. We will also place two dimensions.

Placing Text:

1. Open **Lake Cabin.rvt** created in exercise 2-4.

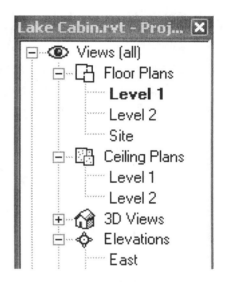

**Figure 2-20** Project Browser

2. Make sure your current view is **Level 1**. The word Level 1 will be bold under the heading *Floor Plans* in your *Project Browser*. If Level 1 is not current, simply double-click on the Level 1 text in the *Project Browser*. (Figure 2-20)

3. Select the **Text** tool under the *Basics* tab in the *Design Bar*.

Once again, notice the Options Bar has changed to display some text options. (Figure 2-21)

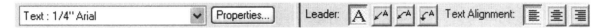

**Figure 2-21** Options Bar for Text tool

The *Type Selector* indicates the text size. From this options bar you can also place text with arrow lines (leaders) and set the text alignment (i.e., Right justified, Centered or Left justified). We will not adjust these setting at this time. *Settings are: no leader & left justified.*

4. You will now place the words Living Room. Click within the living room area to place the text. (Figure 2-22)

5. Type **Living Room**, then click somewhere in the plan view to finish the text.

We notice that the text seems too large. This is a good time to explain what the text height is referring to in the *Type Selector*.

The text height, in the Type Selector, refers to the size of the text on a printed piece of paper. For example, if you print your plan you should be able to place a ruler on the text and read ¼" when the text is set to ¼" in the *Type Selector*.

This can be a complicated process in other CAD programs; Revit makes it very simple. All you need to do is change the **view scale** for **Level 1** and Revit automatically adjusts the text and annotation the match that scale. Currently our view scale is set to 1/8" = 1'-0"; we want the view scale to be 1/4" = 1'-0". With the view scale set to 1/8" 1'-0" our text is twice as big as it should be. Next you will change the view scale for Level 1.

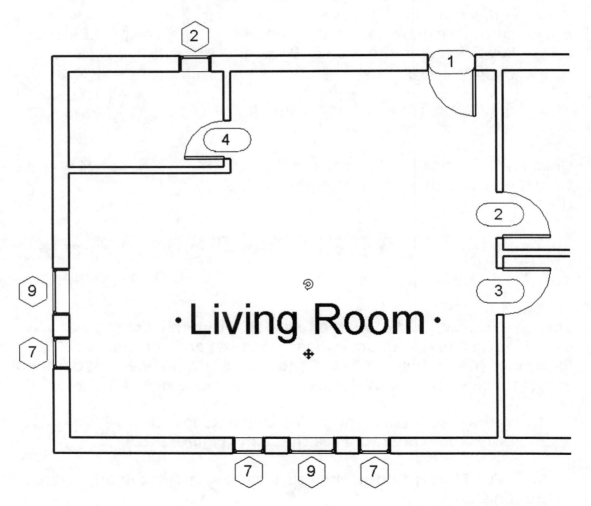

**Figure 2-22** Placing text

6. In the *Project Browser*, **right-click on Level 1** under *Floor Plans*. Select **Properties** from the pop-up menu.

7. In the *Element Properties* dialog, select the Value field for the View Scale Parameter. (Figure 2-23)

8. Click the down arrow that appeared next to the current scale (the current scale should be 1/8" = 1'-0"); now select **1/4" = 1'-0"**.

9. Click **OK**.

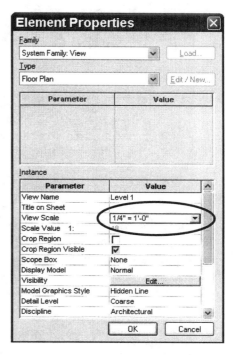

**Figure 2-23** Properties for Level 1

You should now notice that your text and even your door and window symbols are half the size the used to be. (Figure 2 -24)

10. Finally, using the **Text** tool, place a room name label in each room as shown in **Figure 2-1** and **Figure 2-24** below.

11. **Save** your project.

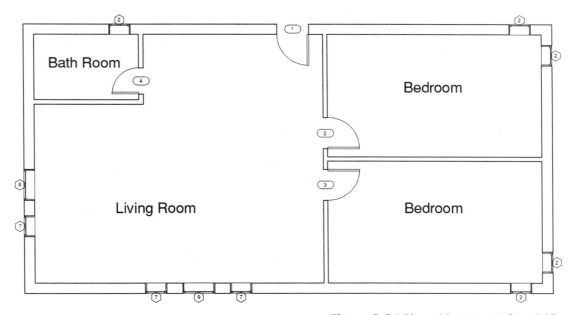

**Figure 2-24** Plan with text at ¼" = 1'-0"

## Place Dimensions:

To finish this exercise we will place two overall dimensions in our plan.

12. Select the **Dimension** tool under the *Basics* tab in the *Design Bar*.

13. In the *Options Bar*, change the drop-down list that says *Prefer wall centerlines* to **Prefer wall faces**. This option will allow you to dimension to the outside face of your building, as you would normally do when dimensioning the overall footprint of your building.

14. Place a dimension by selected two walls and then clicking a third point to specify where the dimension line should be relative to the walls. (Figure 2-25)

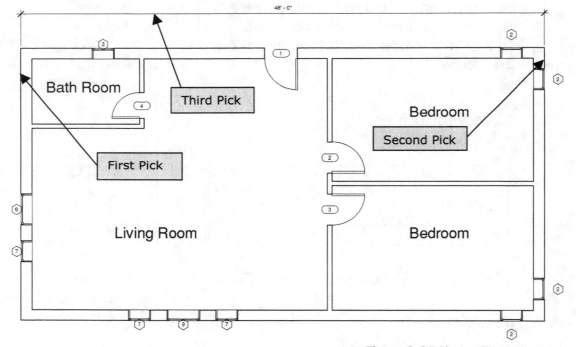

**Figure 2-25** Placing Dimensions

15. Place one more dimension indicating the depth of the building. (Figure 2-1)

16. **Save** your project.

## Exercise 2-6:
## Printing

The last thing you need to know to round off your basic knowledge of Revit is how to print the current view.

Printing the current view:

1.  Select **File → Print** from the menu bar.

2.  Adjust your setting to match those shown in **Figure 2-26**.

    *   Selecting a printer from the list that you have access to.
    *   Set Print Range to: Visible portion of current window

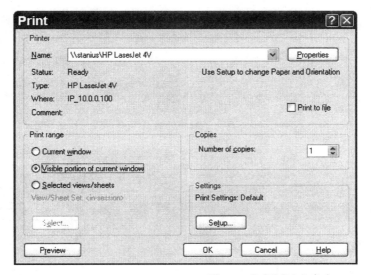

**Figure 2-26** Print dialog

3.  Click on the **Setup** button to adjust additional print settings.

4.  Adjust your setting to match those shown in **Figure 2-27**.

    *   Set Zoom to:
        **Fit to page**

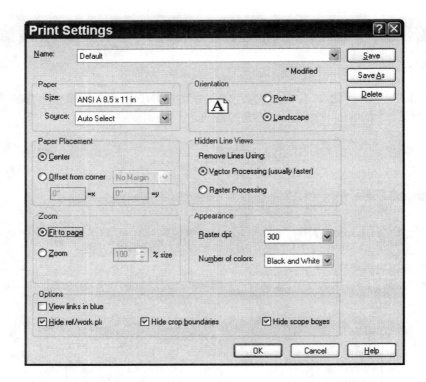

**Figure 2-27** Print Settings dialog

5. Click **OK**.

6. You will see a prompt asking if you want to save the modified "Print Setup." (Figure 2-28) Click **NO**.

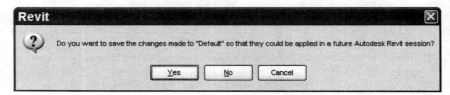

**Figure 2-28** Save print setup

7. Click the **Preview button** in the lower left corner. This will save paper and time by verifying the drawing will be correctly positioned on the page.

8. Click the **Print button** at the top of the preview window

9. Click **OK** to print to the selected printer.

**fyi:**

Notice you do not have the option to set the scale (i.e. 1/8" = 1'-0"). If you recall from our previous exercise the scale is set in the properties for each view.

If you want a quick half-scale print you can change the zoom factor to 50%. You could also select Fit to page to get the largest image possible but not to scale.

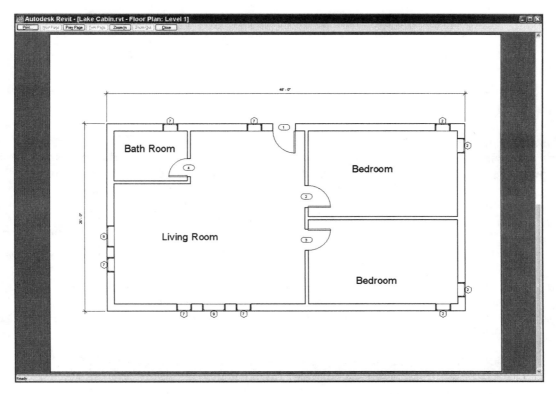

**Figure 2-29** Print Preview

## Self-Exam:

The following questions can be used as a way to check your knowledge of this lesson. The answers can be found on the last page of this section.

1.  The Tape Measure tool is used to dimension drawings. (T/F)

2.  Revit will automatically trim the wall lines when you place a door. (T/F)

3.  Snap will help you to draw faster & more accurately. (T/F)

4.  A 6'-8" door is a standard door height in _____ construction.

5.  While using the wall tool, the height can be quickly adjusted in the

    _____ bar.

## Review Questions:

The following questions may be assigned by your instructor as a way to assess your knowledge of this section. Your instructor has the answers to the review questions.

1.  The **view scale** for a drawing is set by right-clicking on that views label in the Project Browser and selecting Properties. (T/F)

2.  Dimensions are placed with only two clicks of the mouse. (T/F)

3.  The relative size of text in a drawing is controlled by the view scale. (T/F)

4.  You can quickly switch to a different view by double-clicking on that views label in the Project Browser. (T/F)

5.  You cannot select which side of the wall a window is offset to. (T/F)

6.  The _____ key cycles through the available snaps near you cursor.

7.  The _____ tool can be used to list the distance between two walls without drawing a dimension.

8.  While in the Door tool you can change the door style and size in the

    _____ _____ within the Options Bar.

# Lesson 3
# Office Building: FLOOR PLAN  (First Floor)::

In this lesson you will draw the first floor plan of an office building. The office building will be further developed in subsequent chapters. It is recommended that you send adequate time on this lesson as later lessons build on this one.

---

## Exercise 3-1:
## Project overview

---

A program statement is created in the pre-design phase of a project. Working with the client (or user group), the architect gathers as much information as possible about the project before starting to design.

The information gathered includes;
- <u>Rooms</u>:        What rooms are required?
- <u>Size</u>:          How big the rooms need to be? (E.g., toilets for a convention center are much bigger than for a dentists office.)
- <u>Adjacencies</u>:  This room needs to be next to that room. (E.g. the public toilets need to be accessible from the public lobby.)

With the project statement in hand, the architect can begin the design process. Although modifications may (and will) need to be made to the program statement, it is used as a goal to meet the client's needs.

You will not have a program statement, per se, with this project. However, the same information will be provided via step-by-step instructions in this book.

## Project overview:

You will model a three-story office building located in a rural setting. Just to the north of the building site is a medium-sized lake. For the sake of simplicity, the property is virtually flat.

The main entry and parking is from the south side of the building. You enter the building into a three-story atrium. Levels 2 & 3 have guard railings that look down into level 1 in the atrium. The atrium is enclosed on three sides by full height curtain wall (glass walls). See the cover image.

This building is not meant to meet any particular building code. It is strictly a tool to learn how to use Revit. Having said that, however, there are several general comments as to how codes may impact a particular part of the design.

The floor plans are mostly open office areas with a few smaller rooms for toilets, private offices, work & break rooms, etc. These areas have several "punched" window openings on the exterior walls (punched as opposed to ribbon windows).

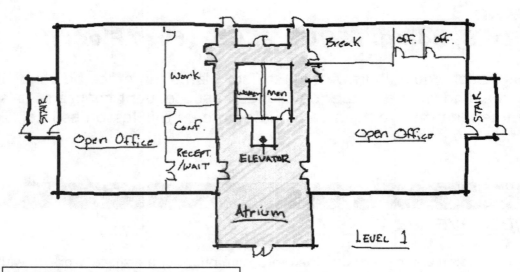

**Figure 3-0a** Level 1 floor plan sketch

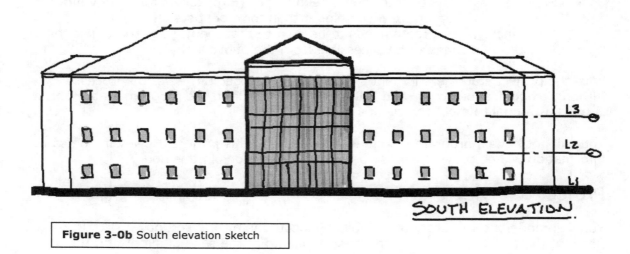

**Figure 3-0b** South elevation sketch

TIP: The two sketches above (Figures 3-0a & 3-0b) were drawn using the new **Autodesk Architectural Studio 3.0** and LCD Display Tablet. Architectural Studio allows you to draw freehand with various (user defined) markers and pencils. The LCD Display Tablet (by Wacom) allows you to draw directly on the LCD display. Some programs, like Photoshop, are pressure sensitive; meaning, the harder you press the pen, the thicker the line that is drawn.

## Exercise 3-2:
## Exterior Walls

You will begin the first floor plan by drawing the exterior walls. Like many projects, early on you might not be certain what the exterior walls are going to be. So, we will start out using the generic wall styles. Then we will change them to a custom wall style (that you will create) once we have decided what the wall construction is.

Adjust wall settings:

1.   Select **Wall** form the Design Bar

2.   Make the following changes to the wall options in the *Options Bar*: (Figure 3-1)
     • Wall style: **Basic Wall: Generic – 12"**
     • Height: **Explicit**
     • Height: **36' 0"**
     • Loc Line: **Finish Face; Exterior**

**Figure 3-1** Option bar: Walls

Draw the exterior walls:

3.   Draw the walls shown in Figure 3-2. Make sure your dimensions are correct. Use the Tape Measure tool if you need additional lengths listed. *Note: if you draw in a clockwise fashion, your walls will have the exterior side of the wall correctly positioned. You can also use the spacebar to toggle which side the exterior face is on.*

TIP: In the Options Bar, while you are in the Wall tool, you can click Chain to continuously draw walls. When Chain is not selected you have to pick the same point twice: once where the line ends and again where the next line begins.

The icons to the right of Chain allow you to specify what shape wall you wish to draw.

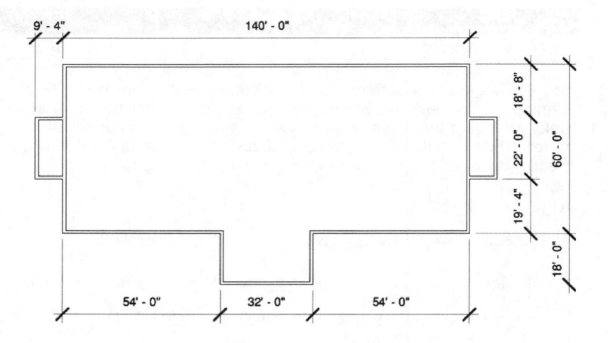

**Figure 3-2** Exterior walls

## Create a custom wall style:

Revit provides several predefined wall styles, from metal studs with gypsum board to concrete block and brick cavity walls. However, you will occasionally need a wall style that has not yet been predefined by Revit. You will study this feature next.

First, you will take a quick look at a more complex wall type that Revit provides so you can see how they are set up.

4.  With the *Wall* tool selected, pick the wall type: **Basic Wall: Exterior – Brick on CMU**, from the *Type Selector* drop-down list.

5.  Click the **Properties** button to the right of the *Type Selector*.

6.  You are now in the *Element Properties* dialog box. Click the **Edit / New** button. (Figure 3-3)

7.  You should be in the *Type Properties* dialog box. Click the **Edit** button next to the *Structure* parameter. (Figure 3-4)

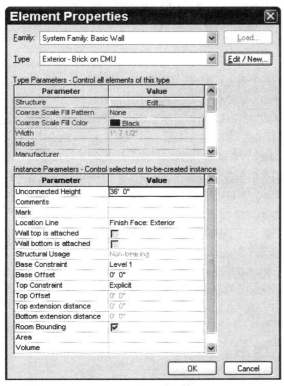

**Figure 3-3** Element Properties

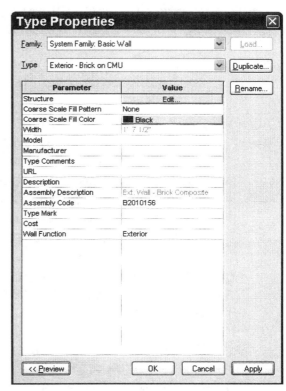

**Figure 3-4** Type Properties

8.   Finally, you are in the *Edit Structure* dialog box. This is where you can modify existing wall types or create new ones. Click **Preview>>** to display a preview of the selected wall type. (Figure 3-5)

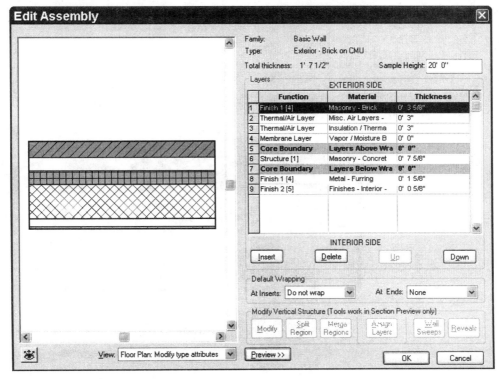

**Figure 3-5** Edit Structure

Here, the *Edit Structure* dialog box allows you to change the composition of an existing wall or (similar) to create a new wall.

Things to notice (Figure 3-5):
- The exterior side is labeled at the top and interior side at the bottom.
- You will see horizontal lines identifying the core material. The core material can be used to place walls and dimension walls. For example: the wall tool will let you draw a wall with the interior or exterior core face as the reference line. On an interior wall you would typically dimension to the face of CMU rather than to the finished face of gypsum board. This is to work out coursing and give the contractor the information needed for the part of the wall he will build first.
- Each row is called a layer. By clicking on a layer and picking the **Up** or **Down** buttons, you can reposition materials within the wall assembly.

9.  Click Cancel in each open dialog box to close them.

10. Set the Wall Style back to **Basic Wall: Generic – 12"** in the type selector.

11. Click the **Properties** button next to the type selector.

12. Click the **Edit / New** button.

13. Click **Duplicate.**

14. Enter Brick & CMU cavity wall for the new wall type name. (Figure 3-6)

**Figure 3-6** New wall type name

Using the **Insert** button and the **Up** and **Down** buttons, add the *layers* to your new wall style as shown below in **Figure 3-7**.

| Function | Material | Thickness |
|---|---|---|
| Finish 1 [4] | Masonry -Brick | 4" |
| Thermal/Air Layer | Misc. Air Layers – Air Space | 2" |
| Thermal/Air Layer | Insulation / Thermal Barriers – Rigid Insulation | 2" |
| *Core Boundary* | *Layers above wrap* | *0"* |
| Structure [1] | Masonry – Concrete Masonry Units | 8" |
| *Core Boundary* | *Layers below wrap* | *0"* |
| Finish 1 [4] | Metal – Stud Layer | 2 1/2" |
| Finish 2 [5] | Finishes – Interior – Gypsum Wall Board | 5/8" |

**Figure 3-7** New wall layers

Masonry is typically drawn nominally in plans and smaller scaled details. This helps to figure out coursing for both drawing and dimensioning. For example, 8" concrete block is actually 7 5/8".

Also, notice that the CMU, Rigid Insulation, Air Space & Brick add up to 16" in thickness. This portion of the wall would sit on a 16" concrete block (CMU) foundation wall directly below.

15. Your dialog should look like **Figure 3-8**. Click **OK** to close all dialog boxes.

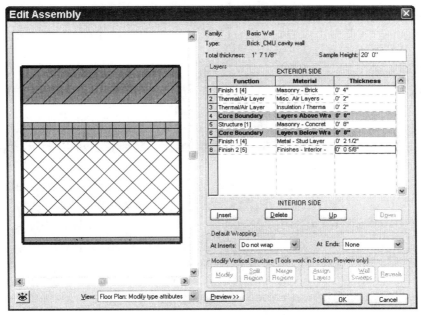

**Figure 3-8** Edit Structure for new wall type

The next step is to change the wall type for the walls previously drawn.

16. Select the **Modify** button from the *Design Bar*; this allows you to select objects in your drawing.

17. Zoom out so you can see the entire plan. Dragging your mouse from one corner to the other, make a window over the plan to select all the walls.

18. With the walls selected, pick Basic Wall: Brick & CMU cavity wall from the Type Selector drop down.

---

**TIP:** If, after selecting all the walls, the Type Selector is not active and does not show any wall types, you probably have some other object selected like text or dimensions. Try to find those objects and delete them.

You can also click on the Filter button (located on the Options Bar when objects are selected) and uncheck the types of objects to exclude from the current selection.

---

You should notice the wall thickness change, but the wall cavity lines and hatch are not showing yet. This is controlled by the Detail Level option for each view.

19. Right-click on **Level 1** in the *Project Browser* and select Properties from the pop-up menu.

20. Set the parameter **Detail Level** to **Medium** and click **OK**.

You should now see the brick and CMU thicknesses with hatching. If you did not pay attention when drawing the walls originally, some of your walls may show the brick to the inside of the building.

21. Select Modify (or press **Ecs**); select a wall. You will see a symbol appear that allows you to flip the wall orientation by clicking on that symbol. (Figure 3-9)

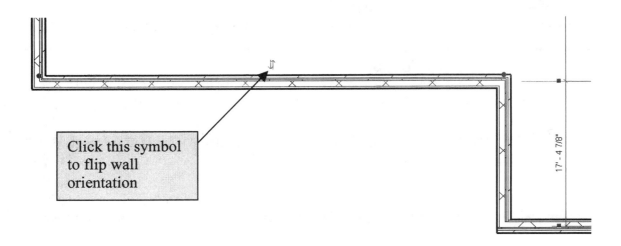

Click this symbol
to flip wall
orientation

**Figure 3-9** Selected Wall

22. Whether you need to adjust walls or not, click on the flip symbol to experiment with its operation. TIP: the flip symbol is always on the exterior side (or what Revit thinks is the exterior side) of the wall.

23. If some walls do need to be adjusted so the brick is to the exterior, do it now. You will probably have to select the wall(s) and use the move tool to reposition the walls to match the required dimensions.

24. **Save** your Project as ex3-2.rvt

---

T**I**P: You can us the MOVE tool ⊢⊩ Move on the menu bar to accurately move walls.

Follow these steps to move an object:
- Select the wall
- Click the Move icon
- Pick any point on the wall
- Start dragging the wall in the correct direction (don't click)
- Start typing the distance you want to move the wall & press Enter.

---

Finally, you will change the three walls at the atrium to be curtain wall (full glass). This will let lots of light into the atrium and better identify the main entry of the building.

25. Drag a window to select the three walls around the atrium.

26. With the walls highlighted, select **Curtain Wall: Curtain Wall 1** from the *Type Selector* drop-down.

Your atrium is now surrounded by curtain wall (Figure 3-10). In a later lesson we will add horizontal and vertical mullions to the curtain wall.

You can see your progress nicely with a 3D view. Click the **Default 3D View** button. Notice that Revit shows the curtain wall as transparent because it knows the curtain wall is glass. The other walls are shaded on the exterior side to make the image read better. You will add mullions to the curtain wall in a later lesson.

27. Save your project as **ex3-2.rvt**

Revit automatically sets the hatch intensity and line weights.

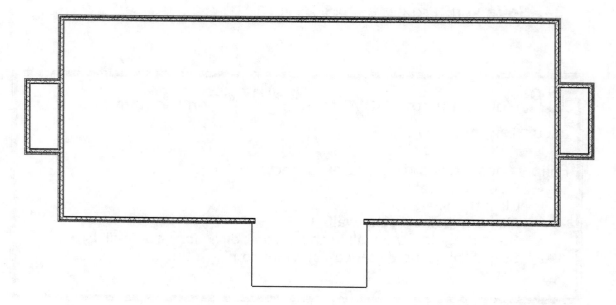

**Figure 3-10** Completed exercise

## Exercise 3-3:
## Interior walls

In this lesson you will draw the interior walls for the first floor.

## Adjust wall settings:

1.  Select **Wall** form the Design Bar

2.  Make the following changes to the wall options in the options bar: (Figure 3-1)
    - Wall style: Basic Wall: Interior – 4 7/8" partition (1-hr)
    - Level: Level 1
    - Height: Level 2
    - Loc Line: Wall Centerline

## Draw the interior walls:

3.  Draw a vertical wall approximately as shown in Figure 3-12. We will adjust its exact position on the next step (step #4).

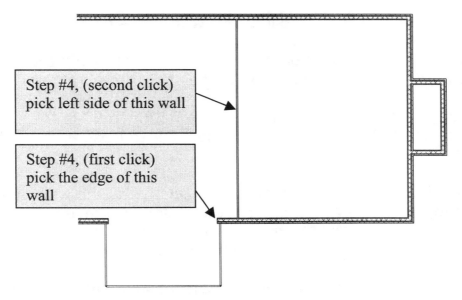

**Figure 3-12** First interior wall

Introduction to Autodesk Revit 5.0

4. Select the interior wall you just drew and use the align tool to align it with the edge of the exterior wall in the atrium (Figure 3-12). When you are done, the wall should look like Figure 3-13.

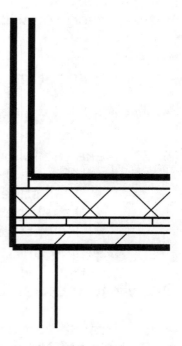 Align

Create the same wall for the west side of the atrium repeating the above steps.

## Modify an existing wall type:

Next you will add some additional interior walls. You will be drawing 8" CMU walls. Revit does have an 8" Masonry wall type available in the default template file that you started your project from. However, the thickness for this wall type is 7 5/8", which is the actual size of a block. Floor plans are always drawn nominally (i.e., 8") not actual (7 5/8"). This is done so you can figure out coursing so minimal cutting is required. Therefore, rather than creating a new wall type you can simply modify the existing wall type.

**Figure 3-13** First interior wall

5. Select the wall style: Basic **Wall: Generic – 8" Masonry**.

6. Click on the **properties** button, and then select the **Edit/New** button. Finally click **Edit** next to the structure parameter.

7. Change the masonry thickness from 7 5/8" to **8"** in the edit structure dialog box, and then select **OK** to close each dialog.

Occasionally Revit will not list dimensions, relative to the walls you want to draw new walls from, while in the create wall mode. One way to deal with this is to draw temporary walls to use as a reference. After using the temporary wall as a reference you can delete it.

8. With the 8" Masonry wall as the current wall, set the location line (Loc. Line) to **Core Centerline**.

9.  Draw the vertical wall shown in Figure 3-14, be sure to snap to the midpoint of the atrium wall as your first point.

Next you will draw an elevator shaft, centered on the atrium and 35'-0" back (thus the temp. wall).

The inside dimensions of the elevator are: 6'-8" x 8'-8". Because you now the inside dimension you will want to adjust to location line to match the known info.

10. Set the Loc. Line to: *Finish Face: Interior*.

11. Draw the elevator shaft. Make sure the location line is to the inside so your shaft is the correct dimension. Draw the shaft anywhere in the drawing; you will adjust the exact position next.

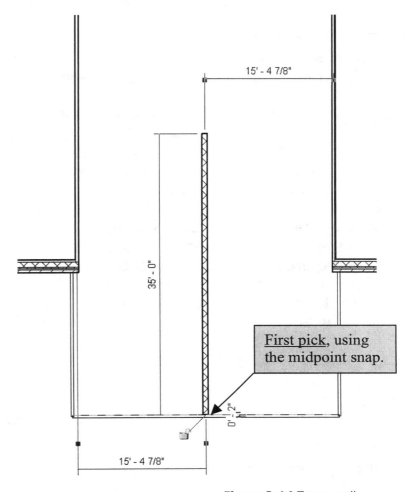

First pick, using the midpoint snap.

**Figure 3-14** Temp. wall

12. Select the 4 walls that represent the elevator shaft, and then pick the **Move** tool.

TIP: Concrete blocks come in various widths, and most are 16" long and 8" high. When drawing plans there is a simple rule to keep in mind to make sure you are designing wall to coursing. This applies to wall lengths and openings within CMU walls.

Dimension rules for CMU coursing in floor plans:
*   *e*'-0" or *e*'-8"  where *e* is any even number (e.g. 6'-0" or 24'-8")
*   *o*'-4"  where *o* is any odd number (e.g. 5'-4")

13. Snap to the mid-point of the shaft as your first point, and then snap to the middle endpoint of your temporary wall (Figure 3-15). You should zoom in to verify your snaps.

The elevator shaft is now perfectly centered in the atrium and exactly 35'-0" back from the south curtain wall.

14. At this point you can **delete** the temporary wall. Select the wall and then right-click and select delete (or press the Delete key on the keyboard).

A temporary wall can be useful for other tasks as wall. One example is the Mirror tool requires a vertical line centered on the atrium to perfectly mirror objects from the east side to the west side of the building.

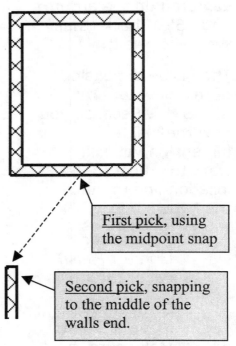

First pick, using the midpoint snap

Second pick, snapping to the middle of the walls end.

**Figure 3-15** Move tool

## Modify an existing wall:

Next we want to change the portion of wall between the building and the east and west stair shafts. To do this you will need to split the current wall, trim the corners and then draw an 8" masonry wall.

15. **Zoom** in on the west stair shaft and select the **Split** tool.

16. Pick somewhere in the middle of the wall. (Figure 3-16)

17. Use the **Trim** tool to trim the corners so the exterior wall only occurs at exterior conditions. *TIP: select the portion of wall you wish to retain.* (Figure 3-17)

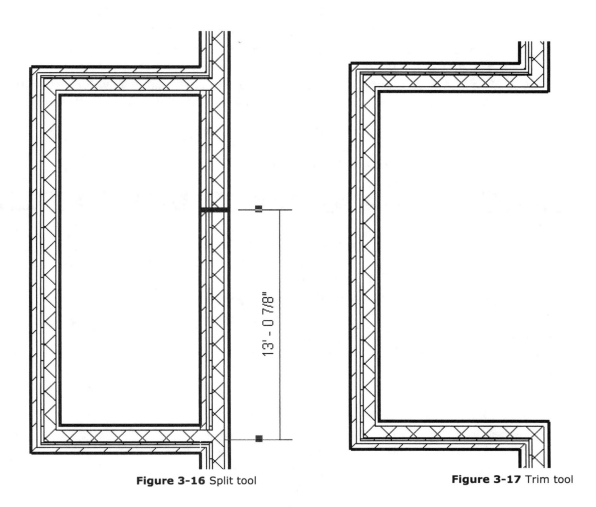

**Figure 3-16** Split tool                    **Figure 3-17** Trim tool

## Additional custom wall types:

We decide that the stair shafts are mostly utilitarian and do not require gypsum board on the walls. In the next steps you will create a new exterior wall type just like the one previously created less the gypsum board and metal studs. Also, you will create a custom wall type to close the open side we created in the previous steps. This wall type will have gypsum board and metal studs on one side.

18. Using wall type: Basic Wall: Brick & CMU cavity wall as a starting point, create a new wall type named **Brick & CMU cavity wall (no GWB)**. Remove the gypsum board and metal studs and save the new wall type.

19. Change the three exterior walls around the west stair shaft to the new wall type created in the previous step.

20. Using wall type: Basic Wall: Brick & CMU cavity wall as a starting point, create a new wall type named **8" Masonry with GWB 1S.** Remove the brick, air space and rigid insulation and save the new wall type. (Figure 3-18)
    **fyi:** it will be useful to come up with a standard naming system for your custom wall types. If the names get to long they are hard to read. The example above has:
    - GWB = Gypsum Wall Board (and would imply studs)
    - 1S = finish only occurs on one side of the wall.

| Function | Material | Thickness |
|---|---|---|
| *n/a* | *n/a* | *n/a* |
| *Core Boundary* | *Layers above wrap* | *0"* |
| Structure [1] | Masonry – Concrete Masonry Units | 8" |
| *Core Boundary* | *Layers below wrap* | *0"* |
| Finish 1 [4] | Metal – Stud Layer | 2 1/2" |
| Finish 2 [5] | Finishes – Interior – Gypsum Wall Board | 5/8" |

**Figure 3-18** New wall layers

21. Draw a wall so the gypsum finish continues on the office side, using the align tool if necessary. (Figure 3-19) Use the measure tool to make sure the stair shaft is the correct size; don't draw the dimensions.

Next you will use the Mirror tool to update the east stair.

22. Erase the four walls of the east stair shaft (this will include the main east wall of the office building). (Figure 3-20)

23. Select the six walls at the west stair. (Figure 3-20)

24. Select the **Mirror** tool and then select the atrium wall identified in Figure 3-20.

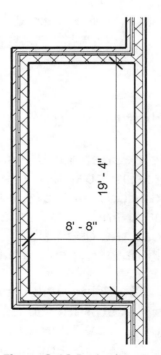

19' - 4"

8' - 8"

**Figure 3-19** Revised west stair

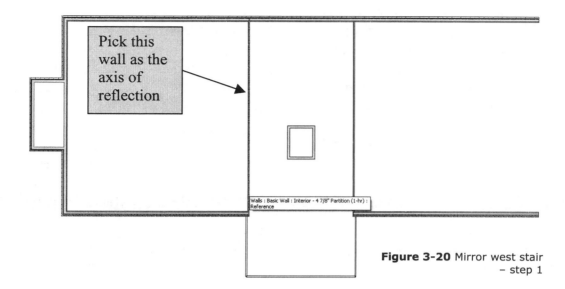

Walls : Basic Wall : Interior - 4 7/8" Partition (1-hr) :
Reference

**Figure 3-20** Mirror west stair
– step 1

25. Use the **Move** tool to reposition the mirrored walls; they should be selected by default. (Figure 3-21)

26. Use the **Measure** tool to verify the overall length of the building is 140'-0". Adjust as necessary.

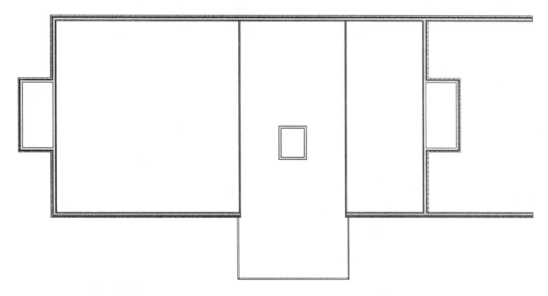

**Figure 3-21** Mirror west stair
– step 2

Finally, you will draw a few more interior walls to compete the first floor plan.

27. Set the Wall style to:
    **Basic Wall: Interior – 4 7/8" partition (1-hr)**

28. Draw the additional walls shown in Figure 3-22. Make sure to position the walls per the dimensions shown. Use the measure tool to verify accuracy. Also, modify the *Loc Line* as required.

**Drawing Tips**: Copy the existing atrium wall 6'-4 7/8" over (6'-0" plus one wall thickness), draw a wall from the midpoint of the elevator shaft w/ centerline reference (Loc Line), and use trim and mirror tools. Do not draw the dimensions. **SAVE YOUR PROJECT as ex3-3.rvt!**

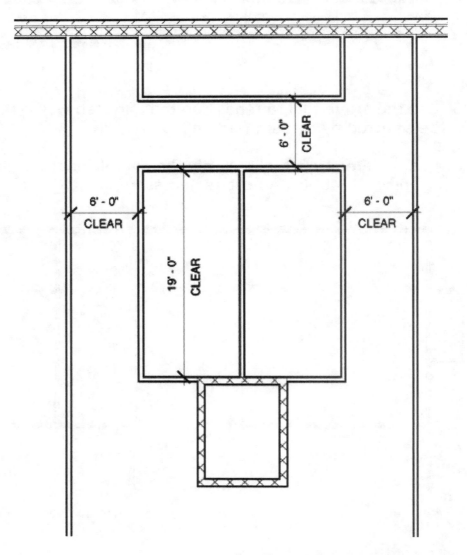

**Figure 3-22** remaining interior walls

## Exercise 3-4:
## Elevator

This lesson will show you how to insert an elevator into your elevator shaft.

## Insert elevator:

Revit provides many groups, which are packages of predefined objects ready to insert into your project. However, many objects are not readily available, like elevators for example. Revit is continually adding content with each new release and to its online library. The online library is where you will acquire an elevator family for use in your project.

1. Open project ex3-3.rvt and **Save As ex3-4.rvt**.

2. Select **File → Load From Library → Load Family...** from the menu bar.

At this point you should see the various categories (folders) available on your local hard drive (Figure 3-23). You should take a minute to explore these folders (just don't click the OK button). You will notice that an elevator is not found anywhere. We will have to download it from the web. *Of course you will need to be connected to the Internet.*

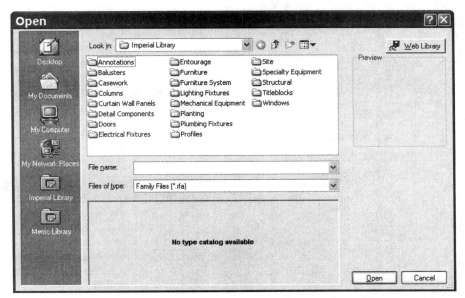

**Figure 3-23** Load groups

3.   Click the **Web Library** button in the upper right. (Figure 3-23)

Revit will open your web browser, then you will be looking at the contents of Revit's FTP (file transfer protocol) site. (Figure 3-24)

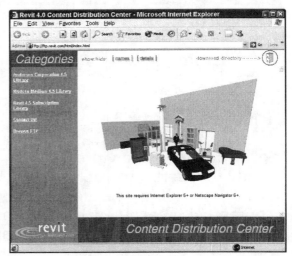

4.   Click on "**Revit 4.5 Subscription Library**"
     *(As of this printing Revit has not updated the label to read 5.0.)*

5.   Click the plus next to **Specialty Equipment**, and then select **Conveying Systems**. (Figure 3-25)

**Figure 3-24** Web content via browser

**Figure 3-25** Web content categories

Within the web browser you should see a graphical representation of each family available for download. (Figure 3-26)

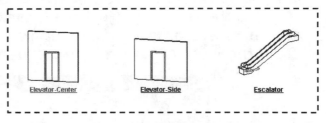

**Figure 3-26** Web content visuals

6.   Click "**Elevator-Center**" to download that family.

7.   Select **Save**. (Figure 3-27a)

**Figure 3-27a** Web browser

8. Save to file to the Desktop using the default name provided.

Now that you have saved the elevator family file to the hard drive, you need to load it into your current project.

9. Select **File → Load From Library → Load Family...** from the menu bar.

10. Browse to the *Desktop* and select the **Elevator-Center.RFA**, and then click **Open** (similar to Figure 3-23).

11. In the Project Browser, click the plus next to Families to expand the list. (Figure 3-27b)

12. Expand the **Generic Models** list, and then **Elevator-Center**. (Figure 3-27b)

As you can see, three elevator types where loaded into your project. Similar to wall types, you can add one of these types as-is, or you can modify or create a new type. You will create a new type to better fit the elevator shaft drawn.

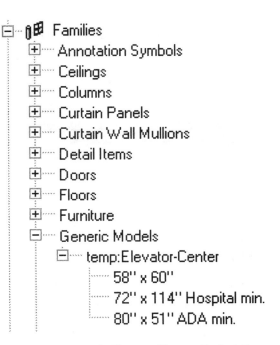

**Figure 3-27b** Elevator library: Project Browser

13. Right-click on the elevator type: **80" x 51" ADA min.**, and then select **Properties** from the pop-up menu.

You will now see a listing of the properties for the selected elevator type. You will use this as a starting point for your custom elevator.

14. Click the **Duplicate** button.

15. Enter the new name: **64" x 84" Car**. (Figure 3-27c)

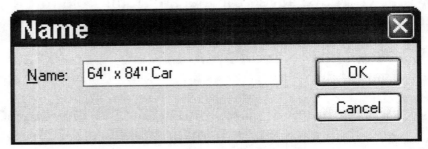

**Figure 3-27c** Elevator type name dialog

16. Click the **Preview** button (if necessary) to see the graphical review of the elevator type, setting the *View* to Floor Plan: Ref. level.

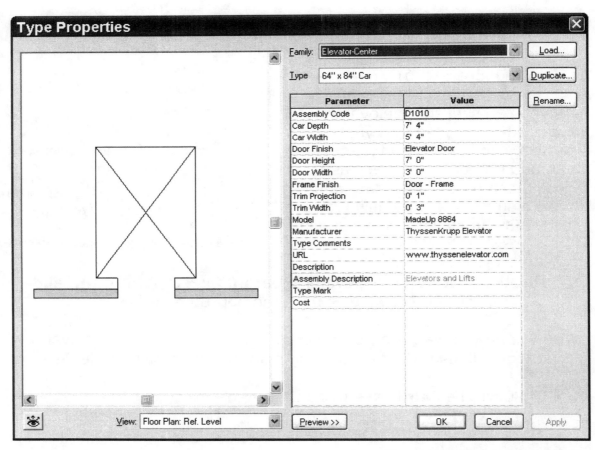

**Figure 3-28** New elevator properties

17. Change or add the following information (Figure 3-28):

- Car Depth: **7'-4"**
- Car Width: **5'-4"**
- Model: **MadeUp 8864**
- Manufacturer: **ThyssenKrupp Elevator**
- URL: **www.thyssenelevator.com**

The last three entries in step 17 are optional (not for this exercise though), but this is a great way to better document the project.

18. Drag the new elevator type from the project browser into the first floor plan. (Figure 3-29)

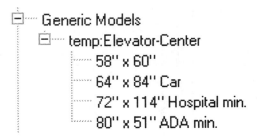

**Figure 3-29** Project browser

The elevator type will be attached to you cursor, ready for insertion.

19. Click within the elevator shaft, and then select the midpoint of the south wall.

20. Select the elevator and adjust the dimensions if necessary to center the elevator in the shaft. (Figure 3-30)

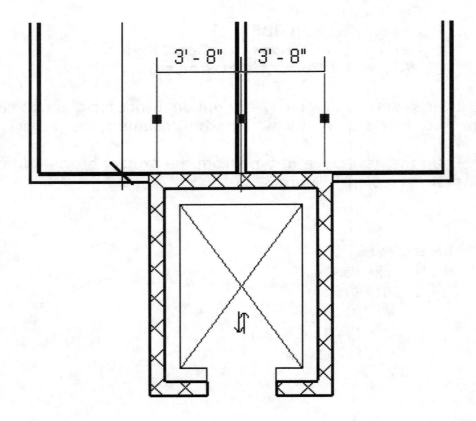

**Figure 3-30** Elevator centered in shaft

Notice when the elevator is selected, the Flip Icon (control arrow) is displayed. Similar to the doors and walls, you can click this icon to flip the orientation of the elevator.

21. Save your project as **ex3-4.rvt**.

## Exercise 3-5:
## Doors and Windows

This lesson will take a closer look at inserting doors and windows.

### Insert doors:

Revit has done an excellent job providing several different door libraries. This makes sense seeing as doors are an important part of an architectural project. Some of the provided libraries include bi-fold, double, pocket, sectional (garage), and vertical rolling, to name a few. In addition to the library groups found on your local hard drive, many more are available via the Web Library feature.

The default template you started with only provides the **Sgl Flush** (Single Flush) group in the Doors family. If you want to insert other styles you will need to load them from the library. The reason for this step is that, when you load a library, Revit actually copies the data into your project file. If every possible group was loaded into your project at the beginning, not only would it be hard to find what you want in a large list of doors, but also the files would be several megabits in size before you even drew the first wall.

You will begin this section by loading a few additional groups into your project.

1. Open project ex3-4.rvt and **Save-As ex3-5.rvt**.

2. With the *Door* tool selected, select **Load from Library** on the *Options Bar*.

3. Double-click on the **Doors** folder. (Figure 3-23)

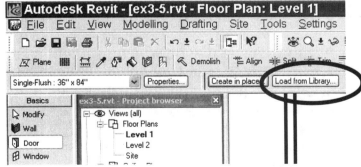

**Figure 3-31** Load from Library

You can now see the door groups available on you hard drive. (Figure 3-32)

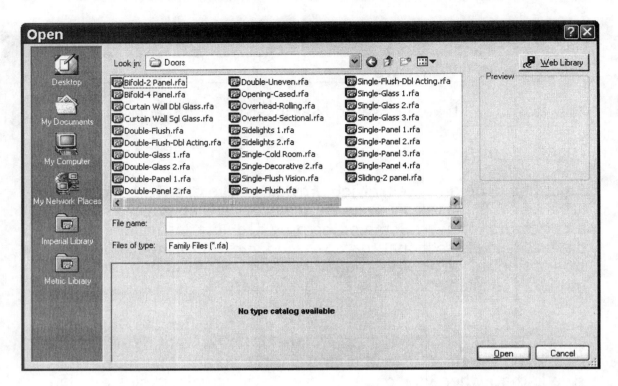

**Figure 3-32** Door groups on hard drive

4.  Select **Curtain Wall Dbl Glass.rfa**, and then click Open.

5.  Repeat steps 2 – 4 to load the following door groups:
    a. **Double-Glass 1**
    b. **Sidelights 1**
    c. **Single-Glass 1**

6.  In the *Project Browser*, expand *Families* and *Doors* to see the loaded door groups. (Figure 3-33)

If you expand the door group itself in the Project Browser you see the predefined door sizes associated with that group. Right-clicking on a door size allows you to rename, delete or duplicate it. To add a door size you duplicate and then modify properties for the new item.

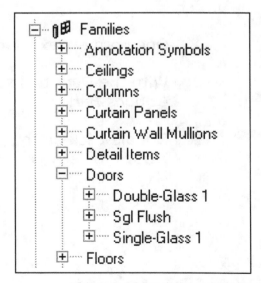

**Figure 3-33** Loaded door groups

Next you will insert the doors into the stair shafts.

7. With the *Door* tool selected, pick **Sgl Flush: 36" x 84"** from the *type selector* on the *Options Bar*.

8. Insert two doors in the west stair shaft as shown in Figure 3-34. Remember you are inserting a door into a masonry wall so your door position and size need to work with coursing. Thus the 8" dimension.

9. Repeat the previous step to insert doors into the east stair shaft.

10. Finish inserting doors for the first floor. (Figure 3-35) Use the following guidelines:

   a. All doors should be 36" wide and 7'-0" tall.
   b. You will not insert doors into the curtain wall for now. You will do that in a later lesson when you design the curtain wall.
   c. Use the style and approximate location shown in Figure 3-35.
   d. Doors across from each other in the two atrium walls should align with each other. Tip: while inserting the second set of doors, watch / wait for the reference line to show up, indicating alignment.
   e. Place doors approximately as shown, exact location not given.

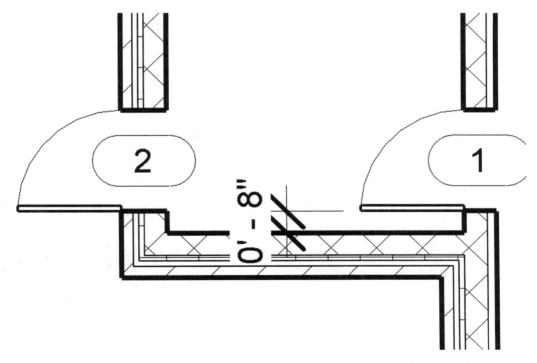

**Figure 3-34** Door in west stair shaft

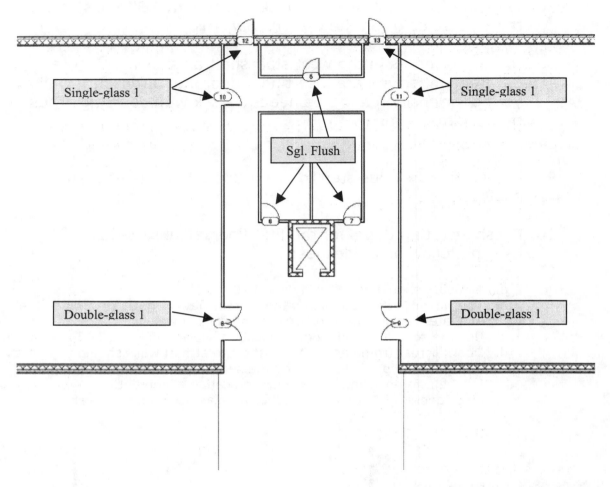

**Figure 3-35** First floor w/ doors

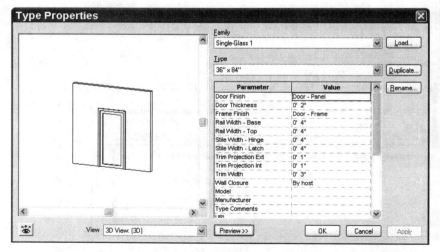

**Figure 3-36** Door properties

## Door Properties:

If you select Properties while the Door tool is active (selected), you can modify various properties related to the door.

You can easily add another standard door size to the Group as required. Click "Duplicate," type a name. (Figure 3-36)

Standard doors sizes (and Groups) can be added to your template file, so you don't re-load it again.

## Insert windows:

Adding windows to your project is very similar to adding doors. Like the doors, the template file you started from has one group preloaded into your project, the FIXED group. Looking at the Type Selector drop-down you will see the various sizes available for insertion. At this point you should also see the SIDELIGHT group that you loaded in the previous exercise. First, you will add a few interior borrowed lights using the sidelight group.

### Interior windows (borrowed lights):

1. With the *Window* tool selected, pick: **Sidelights 1 : 18" x 84"** from the *type selector*.

2. On the west side of the atrium, insert the borrowed lights as shown in Figure 3-37; do not draw the dimensions.

Make sure the borrowed light frames are flush with the atrium side of the wall. You can control that option by moving your cursor to the side of the wall you want the frame flush with before clicking to insert. After drawing the window, you can select the frame and use the flip icon (similar to doors & walls).

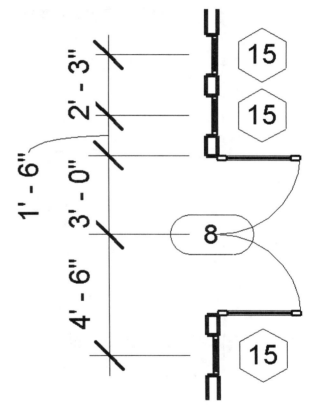

**Figure 3-37** Sidelights added

3. Repeat the previous steps to insert the borrowed lights on the east side of the atrium.

## Exterior windows:

4.  Using the methods previously covered in this book, create a new window size in the *FIXED* family. Create: **Fixed: 32" x 48"**. You are creating this new size to fit coursing in plan view. The largest window (preloaded) that fits coursing in plan view is 24". That is not wide enough for this design.

5.  Adjust the sill height for your new window size to fit within coursing as well. Set the sill height for **Fixed: 32" x 48"** to be 3'-4". (Figure 3-38)

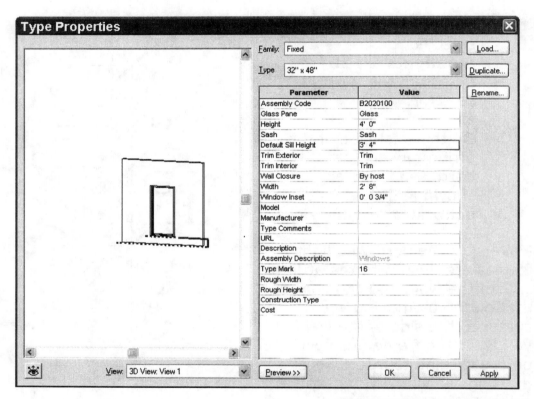

**Figure 3-38** Added window size

6.  Insert the window as shown in **Figure 3-39**. The window should be inserted in masonry coursing.
    **Note:** the dimensions displayed while inserting the window will not work as displayed for coursing because Revit is measuring from the center of the adjacent exterior wall. Thus, you will have to insert the window as close as possible and adjust its location, verifying with the measure tool.

## Array window:

The array tool allows you to quickly copy several objects that Have the same distance between them. You will use array to copy the windows:

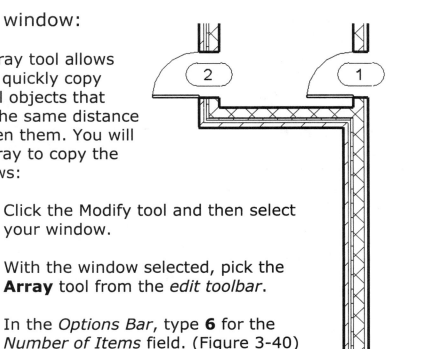

**Figure 3-39** Exterior window

7. Click the Modify tool and then select your window.

8. With the window selected, pick the **Array** tool from the *edit toolbar*.

9. In the *Options Bar*, type **6** for the *Number of Items* field. (Figure 3-40)

10. Click the left mouse button at the midpoint of the window and move your mouse to the east until the dimension displayed is 8'-6".

11. You should now see the windows arrayed in the wall. 8'-6" is not coursing, so select the **Activate Dimensions** button on the *Options Bar* and then enter 8'-8" in the displayed dimension to adjust the window openings. This allows you to more accurately adjust the dimensions.

**Figure 3-40** Window to be arrayed

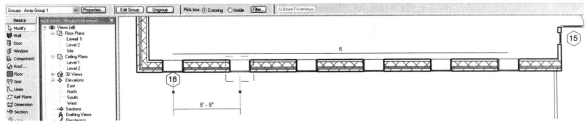

**Figure 3-41** Window after array

12. Set the windows up on the three remaining walls of the first floor. (Figure 3-42) Consider the following:
    a. This would be a good use for the mirror tool.
    b. If you need to create a temporary wall for a mirror reflection axis, make sure the temp. wall is set to centerline.
    c. If drawn accurately, you should be able the use the wall between the two toilet rooms (center, north of elevator shaft) to mirror the windows in the east west direction.
    d. Use the measure tool to verify accuracy.
    e. Use the Ctrl key to select multiple windows.

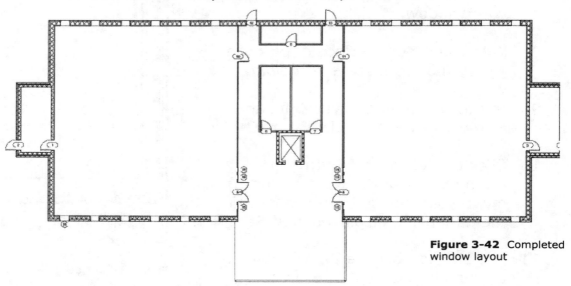

**Figure 3-42** Completed window layout

## Cleaning house:

As previously mentioned, you can view the various Families and groups loaded into your project. The more Families and Groups you have loaded the larger your file is, whether or not you are using them in your project. Therefore, it is a good idea to get rid of any door, window, etc., that you know you will not need in the current project.

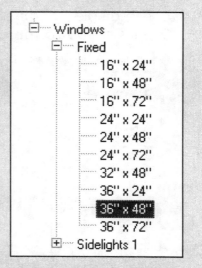

13. In the *Project Browser*, navigate to Families → Windows → Fixed. Right click on **36" x 48"** and select **Delete**.

**Figure 3-43** Project Browser

## Self-Exam:

The following questions can be used as a way to check your knowledge of this lesson. The answers can be found on the last page of this section.

1.  The Option Bar allows you to select which level your wall will be drawn on. (T/F)

2.  It is not possible to draw a wall with the interior or exterior face of the core as the reference point. (T/F)

3.  Objects cannot be move accurately with the Move tool. (T/F)

4.  The _____ tool, in the Design Bar, has to be selected in order to select an object in your project.

5.  A wall has to be _____ to see its flip icons.


## Review Questions:

The following questions may be assigned by your instructor as a way to assess your knowledge of this section. Your instructor has the answers to the review questions.

1.  Revit comes with many predefined doors and windows. (T/F)

2.  The length 3'-8" is a masonry dimension. (T/F)

3.  You can delete unused families & groups in the Project Browser. (T/F)

4.  It is not possible to load families and groups from the Internet. (T/F)

5.  It is not possible to select which side of the wall a window should be on while you are inserting the window. (T/F)

6.  What tool will break a wall into two smaller pieces? _____

7.  The _____ tool allows you to match the surface of two adjacent walls.

8.  Occasionally you have to draw _____ lines to use as a reference point for another object or as a reflection mirror.

9.  You can use the _____ tool to copy an object multiple times in one step.

10. The _____ file has a few doors, windows & walls preloaded in it.


*Self-Exam Answers:*
**1** – T, **2** – F, **3** – T, **4** – Modify, **5** – Selected

**Notes:**

# Lesson 4
# Office Building: FLOOR PLAN (2<sup>nd</sup> and 3<sup>rd</sup> Floors)::

In this lesson you will setup the upper two floors. This will mostly involve copying objects from the first floor with some modifications along the way. You will also adjust the floor-to-floor height and insert stairs into the stair shafts.

## Exercise 4-1:
## Copy common walls from first floor

Setting up the second (and third) floor view:

The first thing you need to do is make a few adjustments to the second (and third) floor settings. The default template you started your project from already has a second floor view setup in the project. The third floor has not been set up, so you will do that.

1. Open Exercise ex3-5.rvt and Save-As **ex4-1.rvt**.

2. In the *Project Browser*, double-click on the **Level 2** view under Floor Plans. (Figure 4-1)

You should now see the second floor plan. Notice that the dark wall lines, shown in this view, exist at this level. The light gray lines are walls for the floor below. (Figure 4-2)

You will turn off the view of the lower level and set the Detail Level to show more detail in the walls.

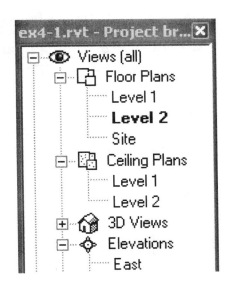

**Figure 4-1** Project Browser; Level 2 view

3. Right-click on the label **Level 2** (under *Floor Plans*) in the *Project Browser*, and then select Properties.

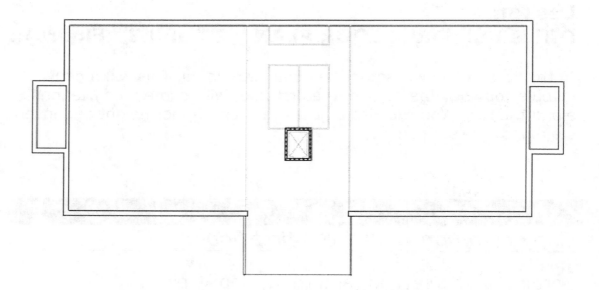

**Figure 4-2** level 2 (Initial view)

4. Make the following adjustment (*Element Properties* dialog):
   a. Detail Level: **Medium**
   b. Underlay: **None**

5. Click **OK**. Your Level 2 floor plan should look like the plan shown below. (Figure 4-3)

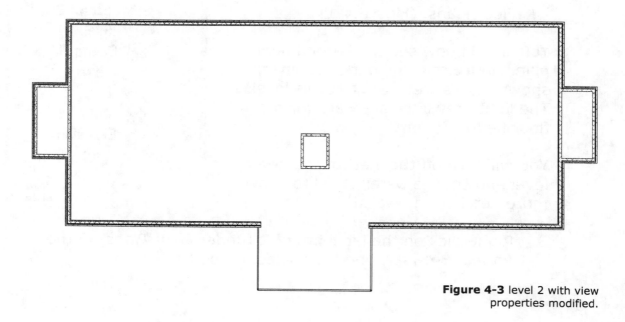

**Figure 4-3** level 2 with view
properties modified.

Because the walls and doors you will copy from the first floor are set up to extend to the floor above, you need to setup the third floor before you copy the walls from first to second (so the second floor walls have a floor to extend to).

Adding another floor is surprisingly simple. You switch to an elevation view and draw in a Level tag. By doing that Revit automatically sets up a Level 3 view in the project browser.

6.  Double-click on one of the four elevation views listed under *Elevations* in the *Project Brows*er. If you do not see your drawing in elevation, try another view and/or see the tip below.

7.  With an elevation on the computer screen, select *Modify* from the *Design Bar* and then select the **Level** tool.

8.  As you move your cursor near the Level 2 symbol you will see a dimension displayed, indicating the distance between Level 2 floor and Level 3 floor you are about to insert. For now, **set Level 3 to be 10'-0" above Level 2**. (Figure 4-4)

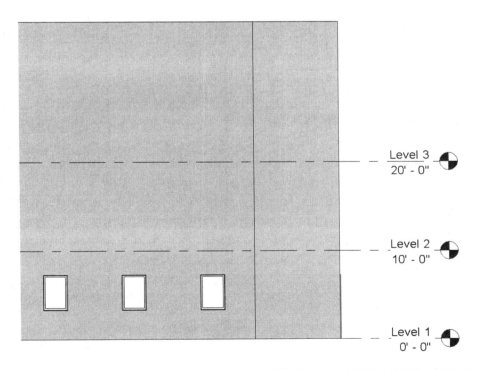

**Figure 4-4** (Partial) South elevation

Notice that the Level 3 floor plan view was automatically added top the project browser.

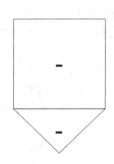

TIP: You have probably figured out on your own what the symbol at the right is for. If not, here it is:

The default template has four Elevation symbols shown in plan view. These symbols represent what the four pre-setup views (under elevation) will see. Therefore, you should start drawing your plan in the approximate center of the four symbols. The symbols can be moved by dragging them with your mouse.

Next you will copy walls & doors from the first floor.

9.   Switch to the **Level 1** view (see step 2).

10.   Select all the interior walls (except elevator shaft), doors and interior windows. Tip: you will need to hold the Ctrl key to select multiple objects with multiple picks. You can drag a window(s) to select multiple objects at once.

11.   With the objects selected, pick **Copy to Clipboard** from the Edit pull-down menu, or **Ctrl + C** on the keyboard.

12.   Switch back to the **Level 2** view.

13.   From the *Edit* pull-down menu select **Paste Aligned →
      Current View**. FYI: paste aligned will make the new objects align with the copied objects below.

Notice the walls, doors and interior windows are now copied to Level 2 (Figure 4-5). We still need to copy the exterior windows and the elevator.

Also, notice that the new doors have different numbers while the interior windows have the same number. Why is this? It relates to industry standards for architectural drafting. Each interior window that is the same size and configuration has the same type number through-out the project. Each door has a unique number because doors have so many variables (i.e., locks, hinges, closer, panics, material, and fire rating). To make doors easier to find, many architectural firms will make the door number the same as the room number the door opens into. You can change the door number by selecting the symbol and then clicking on the text. The door schedule will be updated automatically.

14. Using the same techniques described in the previous steps, copy the exterior windows and elevator to level 2. *TIP*: You will need to ungroup your windows (grouped with array) before copying them. Select one of the windows and pick the ungroup button on the *Options Bar*.

**Why not draw these walls 36'-0" high like the exterior walls and elevator shaft?**

Simulating real-world construction is ideal for several reasons. Mostly, you can be sure shafts align from floor to floor when the shaft is one continuous wall. Although the toilet and atrium walls align, they do not necessarily have to because they are separated by floor construction, this allows one floor to be later modified easily.

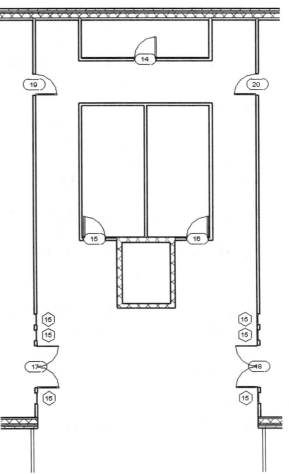

**Figure 4-5** (Partial) Level 2 – walls added

Finally, you will copy the walls and such to Level 3. But first you need to change the height setting for the walls (on level 2), so when you paste them to Level 3 you will not get an error message because there is nothing above (yet) to extend the walls to (e.g., roof or floor).

15. In the Level 2 view, select all the interior walls, doors and windows (except the elevator shaft).

You need to narrow your selection down to just the walls.

16. Select the **Filter** button on the *Options Bar*.

17. **Uncheck** all the items listed except *Walls*. (Figure 4-6)

The list varies depending on what objects are in the selection set. (Figure 4-6)

18. Click **OK**.

**Figure 4-6** Filter dialog

Now only the walls are selected.

19. Select the **Properties** button on the *Options Bar*.

20. Change the *Top Constraint* to **Explicit**, then **OK**.

21. Select the objects again; you can copy the selected objects to the Clipboard.

22. Switch to Level 3, right-click on Level 3 and make the changes listed in step 4 above (e.g., Underlay & Detail Level).

23. Paste the Level 2 objects to Level 3, including Exterior windows and elevator.

24. **Save your project**.

## Exercise 4-2:
## Additional interior walls

This short exercise will help reinforce the commands you have already learned. You will add walls and openings to your project.

Adding walls:

1.  Add the interior walls and doors to Level 1 as shown in Figure 4-7. Use the stud wall you used previously. Use the Align tool to align the walls, which are not dimensioned, with the adjacent walls previously drawn. *(FYI, doors not labeled to be single flush.)*

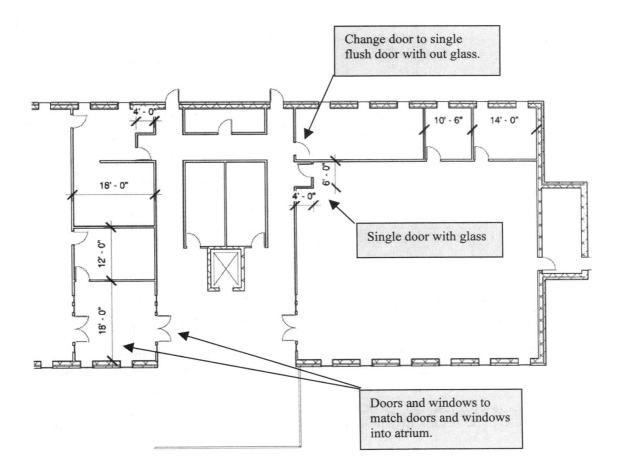

**Figure 4-7** Level 1 Added walls

2.  Similar to step 1, add the walls & doors shown in Figure 4-8 to Level 3.

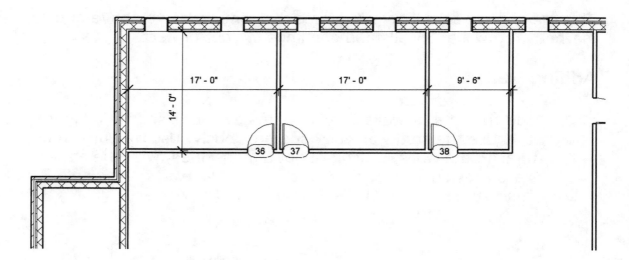

**Figure 4-8** Level 3 Added walls

3.  Use the mirror command to mirror the walls in Figure 4-8 to the other three corners of Level 3.

4.  Finally, modify the small office on the south, each side of building. (Figure 4-9)

fyi:

Your modifications to level 3 included adding a few executive offices to the top floor with the "good" views. You deleted the small office on the south side to make room for a reception desk at the main doors from the atrium. Ideally you would add windows to the interior walls of the executive offices to let borrowed light into the open office area. The center area will be open office area for executive assistants. You will add doors to the stair shaft in exercise 4-4, when you add the stairs.

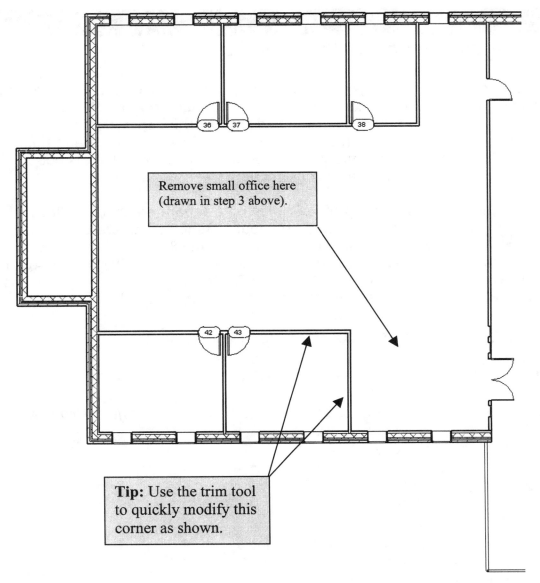

Remove small office here
(drawn in step 3 above).

**Tip:** Use the trim tool
to quickly modify this
corner as shown.

**Figure 4-9** Level 3  Modify walls

5.   Save your project as **ex4-2.rvt**.

## Exercise 4-3:
## Setting the floor-to-floor height

You will modify the buildings floor-to-floor height in this lesson. The reasons for doing this vary. Some examples might be to make the building shorter or taller to accommodate ductwork in the ceilings or the depth of the floor structure (the longer the span the deeper the structure). The default floor-to-floor height in the template file you started from is 10'-0", which is not typically feasibly for commercial construction.

Don't forget to keep a backup of your files on a separate disk (i.e., floppy, CD or ZIP). Your project file should be about 1.33 MB when starting this exercise. At 1.4 MB the file will not fit on a floppy disk. That should not be a problem as most computers today have a CD Burner or a ZIP drive you can use to save large files to. Remember, your Revit project is one large file (not many small files). You do not want anything to happen to it!

## Modify the buildings floor-to-floor height:

1.   Open ex4-2.rvt, Save As **ex4-3.rvt**.

2.   Open the **South** exterior elevation from the *Project Browser*.

Change the floor-to – floor height to be 12'-0" for each level.

3.   Select the floor elevation symbol, and then select the text displaying the elevation. You should now be able to type in a new number. Press Enter to see the changes. Notice the windows move because the sill height has not been changed. (Figure 4-10)

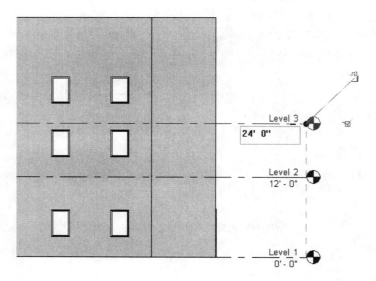

**Figure 4-10** Exterior elevation: modifying Level 3 elevation

4.   **Save** your project.

## Exercise 4-4:
## Stairs

Next you will add stairs to your stair shafts. Revit provides a powerful stair tool that allows you to design stairs quickly with various constraints previously specified (i.e., 7" maximum riser).

### Pre-defining parameters:

Before you draw the stair it will be helpful to review the options available in the stair family.

1. Open ex4-3.rvt and Save As **ex4-4.rvt**.

2. From the *Project Browser*, expand the Families → Stairs → Stair (i.e., click the plus sign next to these labels).

3. Right-click on the stair type: **7" max riser 11" tread**, and select the **properties** option from the pop-up menu.

You should now see the options shown in Figure 4-11.

Take a couple minutes to see what options are available. I will quickly describe a few.

- Tread: depth of tread in plan view.
- Nosing Length (Depth?): Treads are typically 12" deep (usually code min.) and 1" of that depth overlaps the next tread. This overlap is called the nosing.
- Riser: This provides Revit with the maximum dimension allowed (by code, or if you want it, less). The actual dimension will depend on the floor-to-floor height.
- Stringer dimensions: These dimensions usually vary per stair depending on the stair width, run and materials, to name a few. A structural engineer would provide this information after designing the stair.
- Cost: Estimating placeholder.

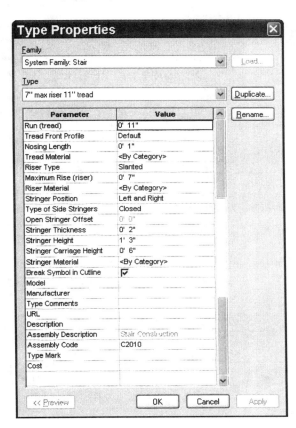

**Figure 4-11** Stair type properties

## Drawing the stairs in plan:

You will be drawing a standard switch-back stair. At first, when using Revit to draw stairs, it may be helpful to figure out the number of risers and landings. That information will be helpful when drawing the stair. As you become more familiar with the stair tool you will not need to do those calculations to draw a stair. Dividing the floor-to-floor height of 12'-0" by 7" we get 20.57. Obviously you cannot have a fraction of a riser so you need to round up to 21 (rounding down would make the riser higher that 7"). Therefore, 12'-0" divided by 21 equals 6.86". Thus you have 21 risers that are 6.86" high. Additionally, most codes would require a landing in a stair rising 12'-0".

4. Make sure you are in the **Level 1** floor plan view.

5. **Zoom in** to the west stair shaft.

6. Click on the **Modeling** tab in the *Design Bar*.

7. Select the **Stairs** tool (on the modeling tab).

8. Click on the **Stairs Properties** button that appeared in the *Design Bar*. (Figure 4-12)

9. Set the Width to **3'-6"**, and then select **OK**. (Figure 4-13)

10. Position the cursor approximately as shown in **Figure 4-14**; you are selecting the start point for the first step. Make sure you are snapping to the wall with *nearest*.

11. Pick the remaining points as shown in Figures 4-15, 4-16 and 4-17.

12. Click **Finish Sketch**. (Figure 4-12)

13. Switch to Level 2 and repeat the previous steps to add a stair from level 2 to level 3.

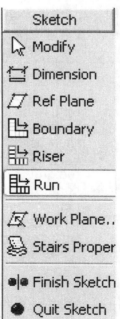

**Figure 4-12**

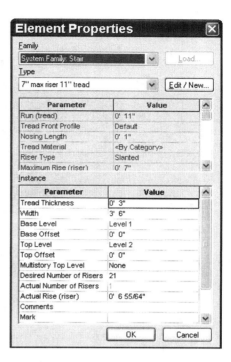

**Figure 4-13** Stair properties

Notice as you draw the stairs, Revit will display the number of risers drawn and the number of risers remaining to be drawn to reach the next level. If you click Finish Sketch before drawing all the required risers, Revit will display an error message. You can leave the problem to be resolved later. Revit will make the stair magenta in color until the problem is resolved.

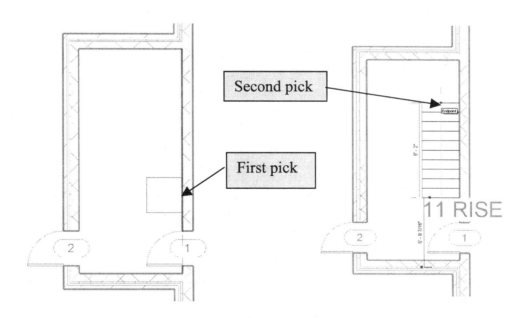

**Figure 4-14** 1st pick     **Figure 4-15** 2nd pick

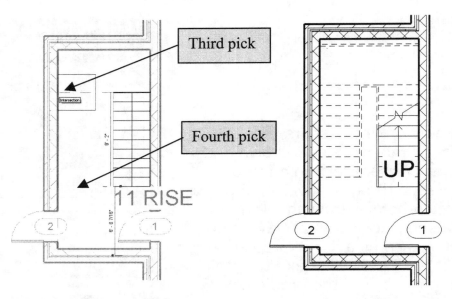

**Figure 4-16**  3rd and 4th picks             **Figure 4-17**  Finished (level 1)

14. Repeat these steps for the east stair shaft.

15. **Add doors** to the second and third floors for both the east and west stair shafts.

16. **Save** your project.

---

FYI: Revit has drawn the intermediate landings between levels.

However, the landings at the main floor levels have not been created. Many projects extend the primary floor structure into the stair shaft to act as the landing for the level and also support the stair. In a later lesson you will draw a floor system that extends into the stair shaft.

## Self-Exam:
The following questions can be used as a way to check your knowledge of this lesson. The answers can be found on the last page of this section.

1. The default settings for the floor plan view shows the walls for the floor below. (T/F)

2. It is not possible to add a new floor level while in an elevation view. (T/F)

3. You should start drawing your floor plan generally centered on the default elevation tags in a new project. (T/F)

4. You can use the Align tool to align one wall with another across a hallway from the other line. (T/F)

5. Where do you change the maximum riser height? _____

## Review Questions:
The following questions may be assigned by your instructor as a way to assess your knowledge of this section. Your instructor has the answers to the review questions.

1. It is not possible to copy/paste objects from one floor to another and have them line-up (with the original objects). (T/F)

2. If a shaft wall is to be built from the lowest level to the roof, and not interrupted at each floor level, the wall should be drawn with that height (not separate walls on each floor level). (T/F)

3. Each Revit view is saved as a separate file on your hard drive. (T/F)

4. You select the part of the wall to be deleted when using the Trim tool. (T/F)

5. You can change the floor-to-floor height by changing the level label (the number indicating distance above level below) in elevation. (T/F)

6. What parameter should be set to none, in the view properties dialog, if you do not want to see the walls from the floor below?

    _____  _____

7. You use the _____ tool create a new floor plan level when in an elevation view.

8. You can use the _____ tool quickly select a certain type of object from a large group of selected objects.

9. The number of _____ remaining is displayed while sketching a stair.

*Self-Exam Answers:*
**1** – T, **2** – F, **3** – T, **4** – T, **5** – Properties

**Notes:**

# Lesson 5
# Office Building: ROOF::

This lesson will look at some of the various options and tools for designing a roof for your building. You will also add skylights.

## Exercise 5-1:
## Hip roof

The first step is to create a floor plan view at the roof level (top of your exterior masonry wall). This will create a working plane for the Roof tool.

## Add elevation symbol:

1.  Open ex4-4.rvt and **Save As ex5-1.rvt**.

2.  Open the **South elevation view**.

3.  Click on the **Level** tool from the *Design Bar's Basic* tab.

4.  Draw a Level symbol at the top of the exterior wall, at elevation 36'-0" – see the wall properties. Draw the symbol so both ends align with the other symbols below it.

Next, you will rename the Level.

5.  Press **Esc** or select **Modify** from the *Design Bar*.

6.  Now select the level symbol you just drew.

7.  With the level symbol selected, click on the text to rename the level label.

8.  Change the label to **T.O. Masonry**. FYI: T.O. means Top Of. (Figure 5-1)

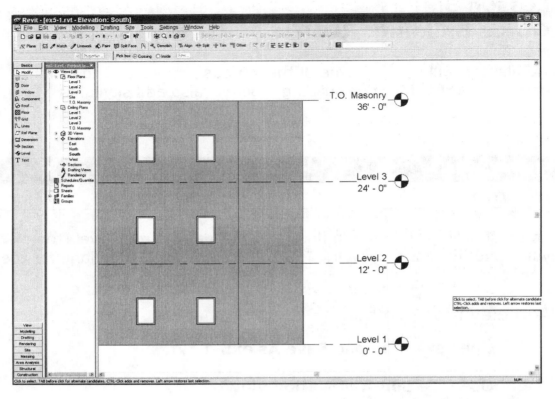

**Figure 5-1** Renamed level symbol

9.  Click **OK** when prompted to rename corresponding views. (Figure 5-2)

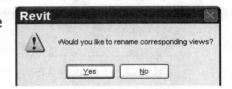

**Figure 5-2** Rename prompt

These steps are the same you used to add the third floor. Notice the "T.O. Masonry" label is now listed in the *Floor Plans* section of the *Project Browser*.

## Add a sloped roof:

10. Open the newly created **T. O. Masonry** view.

11. Select the **Roof** tool from the *Design Bar*.

12. Select "**Roof by footprint**" from the pop-up menu.

Before you start the roof you will change the slope (pitch) of the roof.

13. Click the **Properties** button on the *Options Bar*.

14. Change the **rise/12** to **6"**. Click **OK**. (Figure 5-3)

This will make the roof pitch 6/12, which means; for every 12" horizontally the roof will *rise* 6" vertically.

15. You are now prompted to select exterior walls to define the footprint. Select ONLY the wall segments that define the 120'-0" x 60'-0" portion of the building. (See Figure 5-4) Pick the exterior side of the walls.

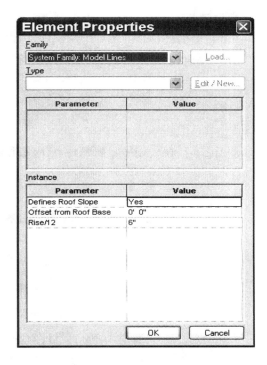

**Figure 5-3** Properties

You will notice in figure 5-3 that there are three sections along the perimeter of the rectangle that are open because no wall is available to pick. You will need to draw three lines to close the "footprint."

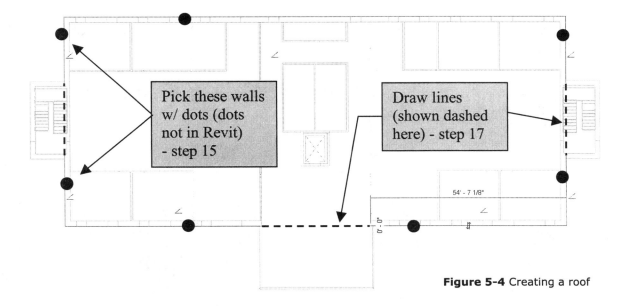

**Figure 5-4** Creating a roof

16. Select the **Lines** tool from the design bar (Figure 5-5)

17. Draw three lines to create a complete rectangle, making sure you use the snaps to accurately snap to the endpoint of the lines already present. (One line across the atrium and the other two at the stair shafts).

18. Now click **Finish roof** from the *Design Bar*. (Figure 5-5)

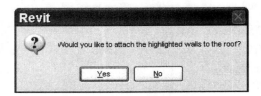

**Figure 5-6** Prompt

19. Click **NO** when prompted to attach the highlighted walls to the roof. (Figure 5-6)

**Figure 5-5** Roof sub-tools

You will now see a portion of the roof in your plan view. The cutting plane is 4'-0" above the floor level, so you are seeing the roof thickness in section at 4'-0" above the T.O. Masonry level.

- Switch to an elevation view to see the roof, south elevation, shown in Figure 5-7.

- You can also switch to the default 3D view to see the roof in isometric view.

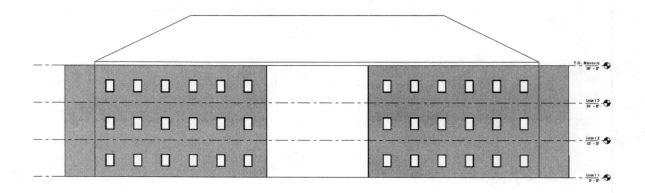

**Figure 5-7** South elevation

After looking at the roof you have created, switch back to the plan view: **T.O. Masonry**. You will now add a roof over the east stair shaft.

20. **Zoom in** on the east stair shaft.

21. Select the **Roof** tool; and click "*Roof by Footprint.*"

22. With **Defines Slope** checked in the *Options Bar*, pick the three exterior walls at the stair shaft.

23. Uncheck **Defines Slope**, and then select the **Line** tool and draw a line as shown in Figure 5-8 to close the footprint. Be sure to use snaps to accurately draw the enclosed area.

24. Pick the **Modify** button and then select the line you just drew.

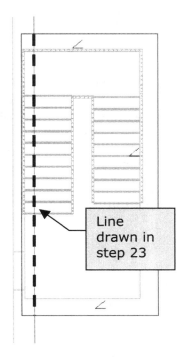

Line drawn in step 23

**Figure 5-8** Roof footprint: east stair

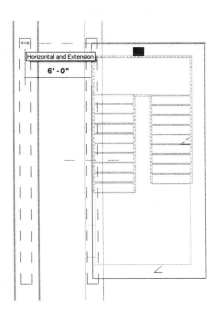

**Figure 5-9** Modified roof footprint; East stair

25. Use the **Move** command to move the line **6'-0"** to the west. (Figure 5-9)

26. Select **Finish Roof** from the *Design Bar*. (Figure 5-5)

27. **Click NO** when prompted to attach the highlighted walls to the roof. (Figure 5-6)

28. Switch to the **south** elevation view. (Figure 5-10)

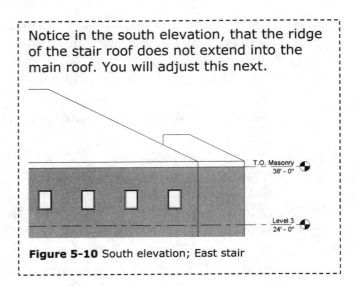

Notice in the south elevation, that the ridge of the stair roof does not extend into the main roof. You will adjust this next.

**Figure 5-10** South elevation; East stair

29. Switch back to the **T.O. Masonry** view.

30. Select the roof object over the east stair shaft.

31. Switch to the **Default 3D View** and Adjust your view to look similar to **Figure 5-11**.

32. Select **Join/Unjoin Roof** from the *Tools* pull-down menu.

You will now select the two edges of the roofs that you want to come together.

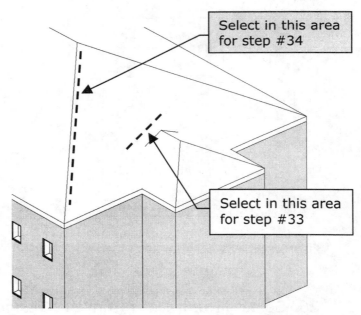

Select in this area for step #34

Select in this area for step #33

**Figure 5-11** Default 3D View

33. Select the edge of the smaller roof – see Figure 5-11.

34. Select the edge of the larger roof – see Figure 5-11.

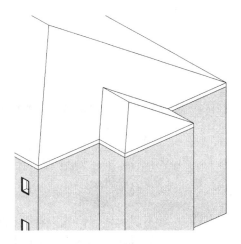

**Figure 5-12** Joined roof

Your roof should now look similar to Figure 5-12. Take another look at the south elevation to see the revision.

35. Repeat the previous steps to create a roof over the west stair shaft.

## Atrium roof:

Next you will create a roof over the atrium area. We want a 4'-0" high aluminum panel above the curtain wall, thus pushing the atrium roof up higher. You will need to create a new wall type for the aluminum panels.

36. Switch to the **T.O. Masonry** view.

37. Select the **Wall** tool and then select the **Basic Wall – Generic – 5"** type.

38. Click **Properties**, click **Edit / New**, click **Duplicate**.

39. Type **exterior wall – aluminum** for the name.

40. Add an **exterior finish** (via edit wall structure) with the material set to **Metal – Aluminum**. (Figure 5-13)

41. Draw three walls, so their exterior faces align with the exterior face of the curtain wall below. Be sure to use snaps and set the wall height to 4'-0".

**Figure 5-13** New wall structure

The walls running north-south need to extend far enough back into the main roof to avoid any holes.

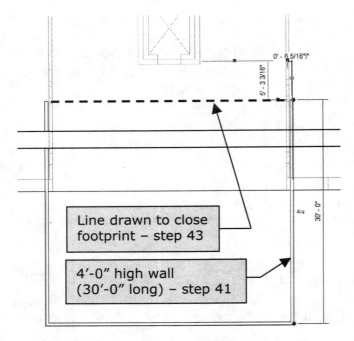

**Figure 5-14** 4'-0" high wall above curtain wall in atrium

Line drawn to close footprint – step 43

4'-0" high wall (30'-0" long) – step 41

42. Use the **Roof** tool to select the three walls just drawn, using the footprint option.

43. Use the **Line** tool to draw a line to close the open side (Figure 5-14). This will create a closed rectangle to complete the roof.

44. Before finishing the roof, select **Roof Properties** and set the **Base Offset** to **4'-0"**. This will place the roof on top of the 4'-0" high wall you just drew.

45. Select **Finish Sketch**.

Your 3D view should look similar to **Figure 5-15**. Like the stair roof, the atrium roof needs to be joined to the main roof.

46. **Click NO** when prompted to attach the highlighted walls to the roof. (Figure 5-6)

47. Use the **Join/Unjoin Roof** tool to join the atrium roof to the main roof.

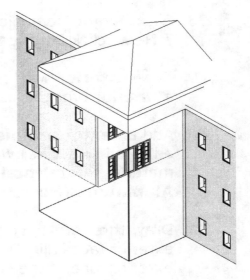

**Figure 5-15** 3D view

Look at the side elevations. If the roof does not extend all the way to the main roof, select the roof and pick Edit Sketch to move the line further into the building. When finished it should look like Figure 5-16.

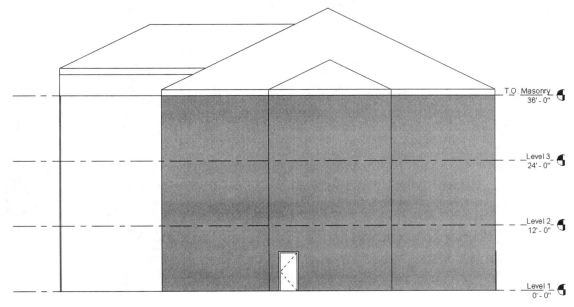

**Figure 5-16** Atrium roof

Next you will take a quick look at the project, thus far, in an isometric view.

48. Click the 3D icon.  3D

The 3D view can be improved by shading the surfaces.

49. Right-click on the **3D** view under *3D Views* in the *Project Browser* and pick **Properties**.

50. Set the **Model Graphics Style** to **Shaded w/ Edges** and then click **OK**. (Figure 5-17)

**Figure 5-17** Setting model graphics style

The 3D Model should now be shaded. (Figure 5-18)

Revit automatically makes windows and curtain walls transparent.

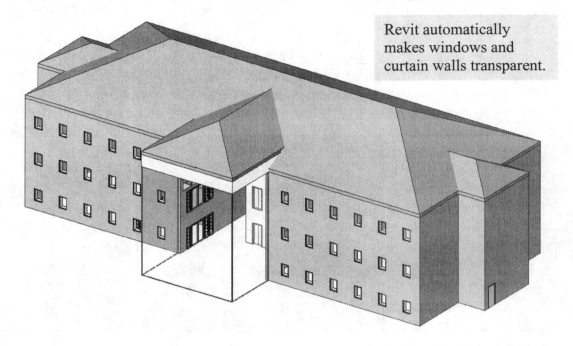

**Figure 5-18** Shaded model

51. **Save** your project.

Try adjusting the view...

## Exercise 5-2:
## Skylights

This short exercise covers inserting skylights in your roof. The process is much like inserting windows. In fact, Revit lists the skylight types with the window types, so you use the *Window* tool to insert skylights into your project.

### Inserting skylights:

You will place the skylights in an elevation view.

1. Load project file **ex5-1.rvt**.

2. Switch to the **South** elevation view.

3. Select the **Window** tool and use the *Properties* button to *Load* the *skylight* group (skylight.rfa) into the project.

4. Select Skylight: 24" x 27" from the type selector. (A 24" wide skylight fits nicely if the trusses are space 24" O.C.)

You are now ready to place skylights in the roof. Revit will only look for roof objects when placing skylights, so you don't have to worry about a skylight ending up in a wall.

5. Roughly place four skylights as shown in Figure 5-19.

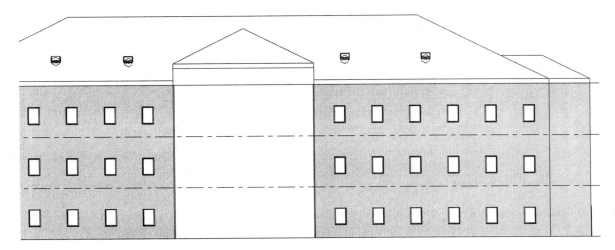

**Figure 5-19** South elevation, skylights added

6.  Press **Esc** or click the **Modify** tool to cancel in *Window* tool.

Next, you will want to align the skylights with each other.

7.  Switch to the **West** elevation view.

8.  Select one of the visible skylights.

You should now have the skylight selected and see the reference dimensions that allow you to adjust the exact location of the object. Occasionally, the dimension does not go to the point on the drawing that you are interested in referencing from. Revit allows you to adjust where those temporary dimensions point to.

9.  Click and drag the grip shown in Figure 5-20 to (wait until it snaps) to the ridge of the main roof (Figure 5-21).

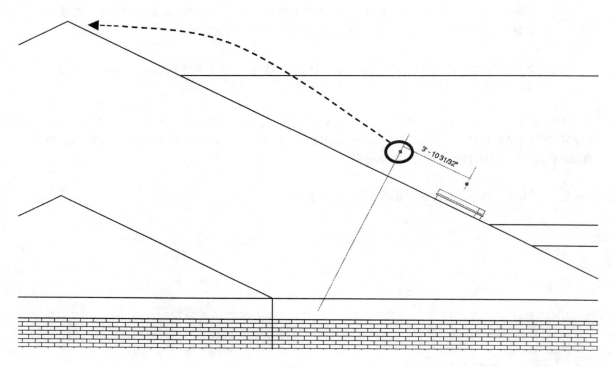

**Figure 5-20** West elevation: default dimension shown when selecting skylight.

10. Click on the dimension text and change the text to **22'-8"**. **Note:** This would adjust the position of the skylight relative to the roof.

11. Select the other skylight on the west elevation and adjust it to match the one you just revised.

12. Switch to the East elevation and repeat the above steps to adjust.

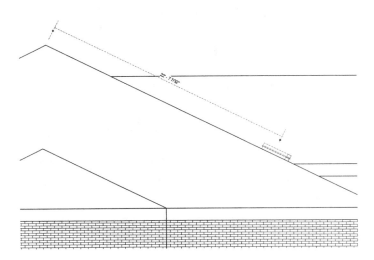

**Figure 5-21** West elevation: default dimension shown when selecting skylight.

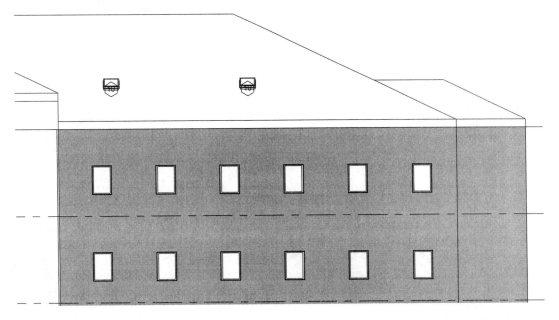

**Figure 5-22** South elevation: with skylights added

You drawing should look similar to the one above. Notice that the skylight tag is right on top of the skylight. You will adjust that next.

13. **Zoom in** on one of the skylights and **click** on the skylight tag (south view).

14. You should see a symbol appear near the bottom of the symbol, Drag on this symbol to move the tag down. (Figure 5-23)

15. Position the skylight tag so the tag does not overlap the skylight. (Figure 5-24)

16. Adjust the other skylights tags, As you reposition these tag you may see a reference line appear indicating the symbol will align automatically align with an adjacent symbol.

Take a minute to look at your shaded 3D view and try changing the view so you can see through the skylight glass into the spaces below. (Fig. 5-25)

17. **Save** as **ex5-2.rvt**.

**Figure 5-23** Enlarged skylight detail

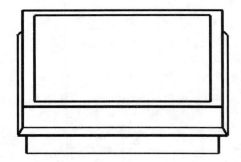

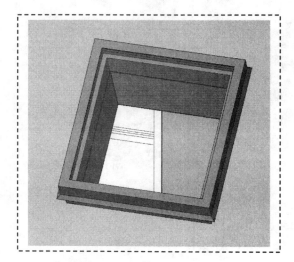

**Figure 5-25** Shaded skylight view

**Figure 5-24** Enlarged skylight detail - revised

## Exercise 5-3:
## Design options (Style, pitch & overhang)

In this lesson you will look at the various ways to use the *Roof* tool to draw the more common roof forms used in architecture today.

### Start a new Revit Project:

You will start a new project for this lesson so you can quickly compare the results of using the *Roof* tool.

1.  Start a new project using the **default.rte** template.

2.  Switch to the North view and rename the level named Level 2 to T.O. Masonry. This will be the reference point for your roof.

3.  Switch to the Level 1 view.

### Draw walls to setup for using the roof tool:

4.  Set the Level 1 "detail Level" to medium, so the material hatching is visible within the walls. *Tip: right-click on Level 1 in project browser & select Properties.*

5.  Using the Wall tool and wall type set to "Exterior - Brick on Mtl. Stud," draw a 40'-0" x 20'-0" building. (Figure 5-26)

*Be sure to draw the building within the elevation tags.*

**Figure 5-26**
Bldg. & Elev. tags

You will copy the building so that you have 4 total. You will draw a different type of roof on each one.

6.  Drag a window around the walls to select them. Then use the copy command to setup four buildings 35'-0" O.C. (Figure 5-27)

**Figure 5-27**
4 buildings

## Hip roof:

The various roof forms are largely defined by the "Defines Slope" setting. This is displayed in the *Options Bar* while the *Roof* tool is active. When a wall is selected, while the "Defines slope" option is selected, the roof above that portion of wall slopes. You will see this more clearly in the examples below.

7.  Switch to the **T.O. Masonry** view.

8.  Select the **Roof** tool, and then **Roof by Footprint** from the pop-up menu at appears after selecting the Roof tool.

9.  Set the overhang to **2'-0"** and make sure *"Defines slope"* is selected (checked) in the *Options Bar*.

10. Now select the four walls of the building at the far left.

11. Click **Finish Roof**.

12. Click **Yes** to attach the Roof to the walls.

13. Switch to the **South** elevation view. (Figure 5-28)

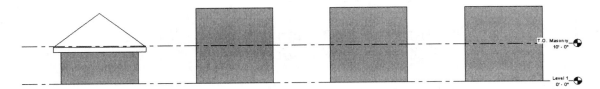

**Figure 5-28**   South elevation – hip roof

You will notice that the default wall height is much higher than what we ultimately want. However, when the roof is drawn at the correct elevation and you attach the walls to the roof, the walls automatically adjust to stop under the roof object.

14. Switch to the **Default 3D** view. (Figure 5-29) You can change the "model graphics style" to shaded if you'd like.

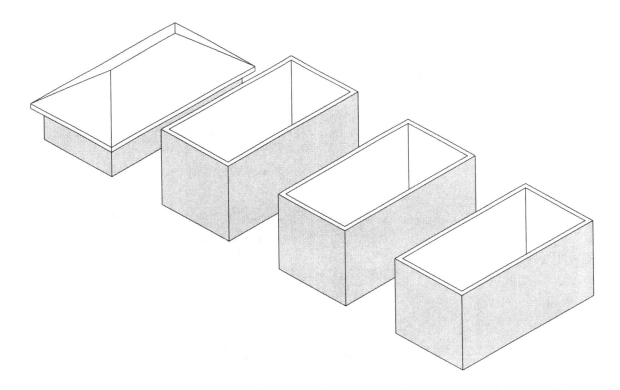

**Figure 5-29**   3D view – hip roof

# Gable roof:

15. Switch back to the **T.O. Masonry** view.

16. Select the **Roof** tool, and then **Roof by Footprint**.

17. Set the overhang to **2'-0"** and make sure *"Defines slope"* is selected (checked) in the *Options Bar*.

18. Only select the two long (40'-0") walls.

19. Uncheck the *"Defines slope"* options.

20. Select the remaining two walls. (Figure 5-30)

21. Pick **Finish Roof**.

22. Select **Yes** to attach the walls to the roof.

23. Switch to the **South** elevation view. (Figure 5-31)

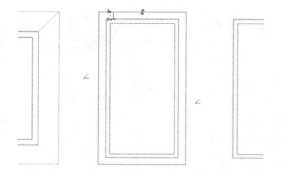

**Figure 5-30**   Gable – plan view

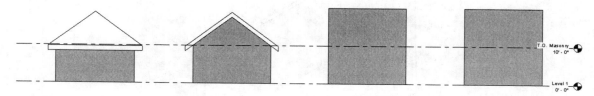

**Figure 5-31**   South elevation – gable roof

24. Switch to the Default 3D view (Figure 5-32).

Notice the wall extends up to conform to the underside of the roof.

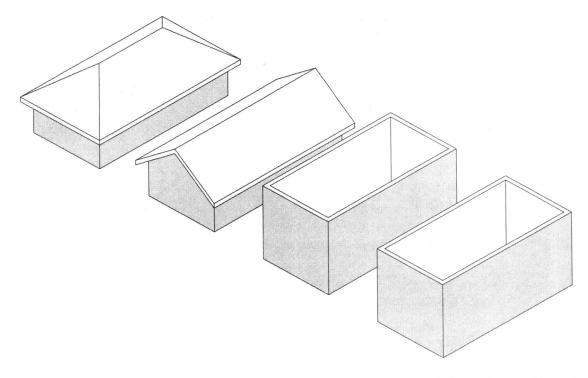

**Figure 5-32**   Default 3D view – gable roof

Shed roof:

25. Switch back to the **T.O. Masonry** view.

26. Select the **Roof** tool, and then **Roof by Footprint**.

27. Check *"Defines slope."*

28. Click on the **Properties** button on the *Options Bar*.

29. Set the roof pitch to 3/12 (Figure 5-33); click **OK**. *FYI: the "Defines slope" option must be selected to change the pitch.*

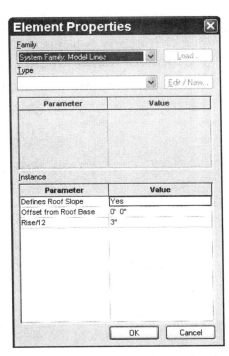

**Figure 5-33**   Properties for roof tool

30. Set the overhang to **2'-0"** and make sure "*Defines slope*" is selected (checked) in the *Options Bar*.

31. Select the east wall (40'-0" wall, right).

32. **Uncheck** "*Defines slope*" in the *Options Bar*.

33. Select the remaining three walls. (Figure 5-34)

34. Pick **Finish Roof**.

35. Select **Yes** to attach the walls to the roof.

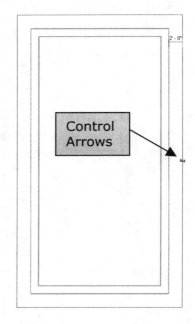

**Figure 5-34**   Selected walls

---

*TIP:* You can use the **Control Arrows** (while the roof line is still selected) to flip the orientation of the roof overhang if you accidentally selected the wrong side of the wall (and the overhang is on the inside of the building. (Figure 5-34)

---

36. Switch to the **South** elevation view. (Figure 5-35)

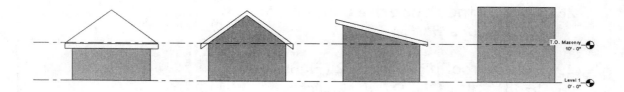

**Figure 5-35**   South elevation – shed roof

37. Switch to the **Default 3D** view (Figure 5-36)

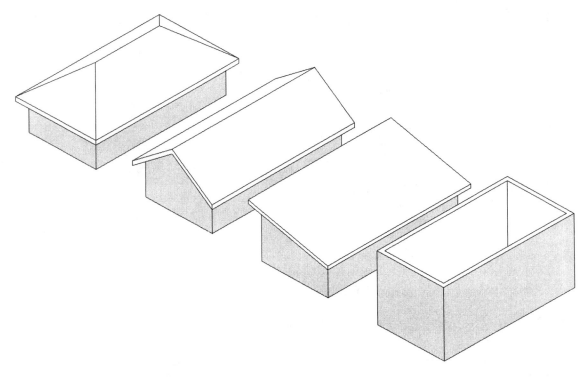

**Figure 5-36**   Default 3D view – shed roof

Once the roof is drawn, you can easily change the roof's overhang. You will try this on the shed roof. You will also make the roof slope in the opposite direction.

38. In **T.O. Masonry** view, Select **Modify** from the *Design Bar*, and then select the shed roof.

39. Click **Edit Sketch** from the *Options Bar*.

40. Click on the east roofline to select it.

41. **Uncheck** *"defines slope"* from the *Options Bar*.

42. Now select the west roofline and check *"defines slope."*

If you were to select Finish Roof now, the shed roof would be sloping in the opposite direction. But, before you do that, you will adjust the roof overhang at the high side.

43. Click on the east roofline again, to select it.

44. Change the overhang to **6'-0"** in the *Options Bar*.

Changing the overhang only affects the selected roofline.

45. Select **Finish Roof**.

46. Switch to the South view to see the change. (Figure 5-37)

That concludes the shed roof example.

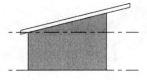

**Figure 5-37** South elevation – shed roof (revised)

## Flat roof:

47. Switch back to the **T.O. Masonry** view.

48. Select the **Roof** tool & then **Roof by Footprint**.

49. Set the overhang to **2'-0"** and make sure "*Defines slope*" is not selected (un-checked) in the *Options Bar*.

50. Select all four walls.

51. Pick **Finish Roof**.

52. Select **Yes** to attach the walls to the roof.

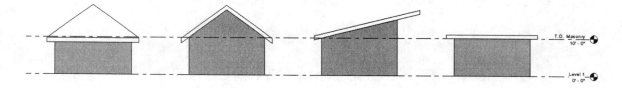

**Figure 5-38** South elevation – flat roof

53. Switch to the **South** elevation view. (Figure 5-38)

54. Also, take a look the **default 3D** view. (Figure 5-39)

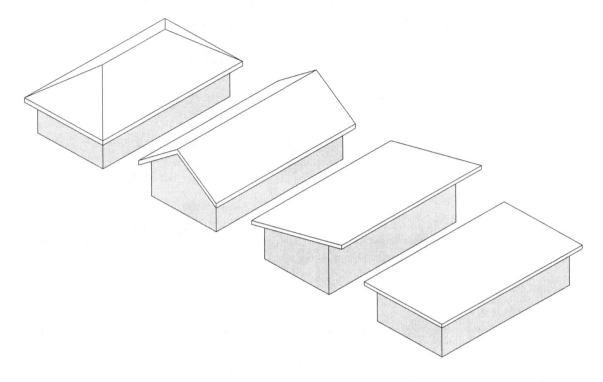

**Figure 5-39**   Default 3D view – flat roof

55. Save your project as **ex5-3.rvt**.

# Want more?

Revit has additional tools and techniques available for creating more complex roof forms. However, that is beyond the scope of this book. If you want to learn more about roofs, or anything else, take a look at one of the following resources:

- Revit **Tutorials** from the *Help* pull-down menu
- Revit **Web Site**
- Revit **Newsgroup** (potential answers to specific questions)

## Self-Exam:

The following questions can be used as a way to check your knowledge of this lesson. The answers can be found on the last page of this section.

1.  You don't have to click *Finish Sketch* when you are done defining a roof. (T/F)

2.  The wall below the roof automatically conforms to the underside of the roof when you join the walls to the roof. (T/F)

3.  The roof overhang setting is available from the Options Bar. (T/F)

4.  To create a gable roof on a building with 4 walls, two of the walls should not

    have the _____ option checked.

5.  Is it possible to change the reference point for a temporary dimension that is displayed while an object is selected? (Y/N)

## Review Questions:

The following questions may be assigned by your instructor as a way to assess your knowledge of this section. Your instructor has the answers to the review questions.

1.  When creating a roof using the "*create roof by specifying footprint*" option, you need to create a closed perimeter. (T/F)

2.  Can The "*defines slope*" setting be changed after the roof is "finished?" (T/F)

3.  Skylights need to be rotated to align with the plane (pitch) of the roof. (T/F)

4.  Skylights automatically make the glass transparent in shaded views. (T/F)

5.  While using the **Roof** tool, you can use the _____ tool from the *Design Bar* to fill in the missing segments to close the perimeter.

6.  You use the _____ variable to adjust the vertical position of the roof relative to the current working plane (view).

7.  While using the roof tool, you need to select the _____ tool from the *Options Bar* before you can select a roofline for modification.

8.  You need to use the _____ _____ to flip the roofline when you pick the wrong side of the wall and the overhang is shown on the inside.

**Self-Exam answers:**
1 - **F**, 2 – **T**, 3 – **T**, 4 – **defines slope**, 5 - **Y**

# Lesson 6
# Office Building: FLOOR SYSTEMS AND REFLECTED CEILING PLANS::

In this lesson you will learn to create floor structures and reflected ceiling plans.

Even though you currently have floor levels defined, you do not have an object that represents the mass of the floor systems. You will add floor systems with holes for stairs, elevators, and the atrium.

Ceiling systems allow you to specify the ceiling material by room and the height above the floor. Once the ceiling has been added it will show up in section views (sections are created later in this book).

## Exercise 6-1:
## Floor Systems

Similar to other Revit objects, you can select from a few pre-defined object types. You can also create new types. In your office building you will use a pre-defined floor system for the two upper levels and create a new type for the first level.

## Level 1, Slab on Grade:

Sketching floors is a lot like sketching roofs (Lesson 5), you can select walls to define the perimeter and draw lines to fill in the blanks and add holes (cut-outs) in the floor object.

1. Open ex5-2.rvt and **Save As ex6-1.rvt.**

2. Switch to the **Level 1** floor plan view.

3. From the *Basic* tab on the *Design Bar*, select **Floor.**

4. Click the **Floor Properties** button on the *Design Bar.*

5. Click **Edit / New.**

6. Click **Duplicate.**

7. Type **6" Slab on Grade**, then **OK.**

8. Click the **Edit** button next to the *Structure* Parameter.

9. Change the material for the structure layer shown to **Concrete: cast-in-place concrete**, and change the thickness to **6"**.

10. Add a layer: **Finish: Interior - Carpet 1**, Thickness **1/4"** (Figure 6-1).

11. Add another layer;
    a. *Function*: **Membrane**
    b. *Material*: **Vapor / Moisture Barriers – Vapor Retarder** (Figure 6-1).

12. Click **OK** to close the open dialog boxes.

13. Select all the exterior walls on **Level 1**, this should include the curtain wall at the atrium and the stair shafts. (Figure 6-3)
    TIP: select the interior side of the wall, you can use the control arrows if needed.

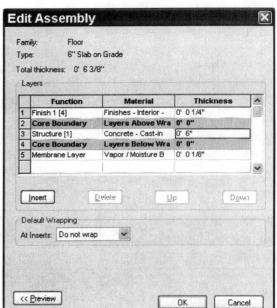

**Figure 6-1** New Floor System

14. Click **Finish Sketch.**

You will most likely get an error message. This is because the main exterior walls extend into the atrium (past the curtain wall). Because this is not a perfect corner (and it does not need to be), you can trim the "edge of slab" lines while in sketch mode to create a true corner, i.e. a closed line. (Figure 6-2)

15. *If you did not get an error skip ahead to step 18)* Click **Continue**

16. Use the **Trim** tool; select the two lines leading to the corner that needs to be trimmed. Do this for both sides of the atrium. (Figure 6-3)

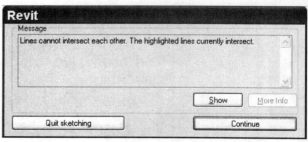

**Figure 6-2** Floor error message

17. Click **Finish Sketch.**

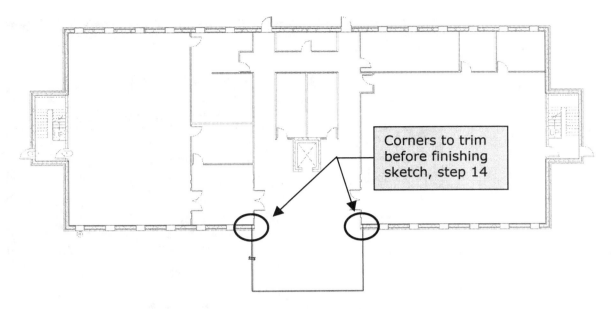

Corners to trim
before finishing
sketch, step 14

**Figure 6-3** Floor creation;
highlighted walls

You now have a floor at the first level. You should see a stipple pattern representing the floor area. You would most likely want to turn that pattern off for a floor plan. You will do that next.

18. In the *Project Browser*, right-click on the **Floor Plan: Level 1** view.

19. Select **Properties.**

20. Select **Edit**, next to the *Visibility* parameter. (Figure 6-4)

21. In the *View Visibility/Graphics window*, click the "plus" sign next to **Roof** in the Visibility column. (Figure 6-5)

22. Uncheck **surface pattern**.

23. Click **OK** to close the dialogs.

The stipple pattern is no longer visible.

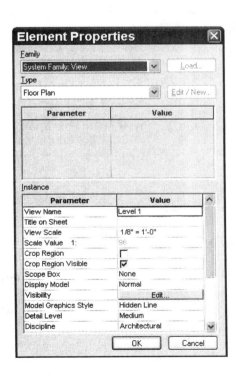

**Figure 6-4** Level 1 view Properties

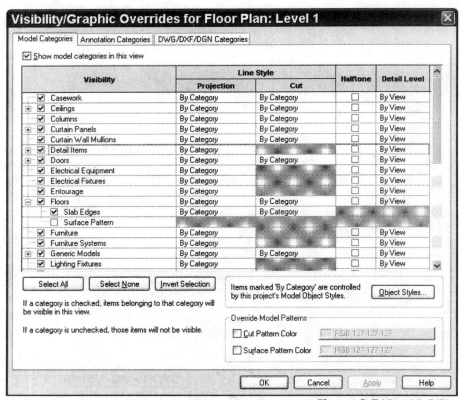

**Figure 6-5** View Visibility

## Levels 2 and 3, conc. + metal deck + bar joists:

24. Switch to **Level 2** view.

25. Activate the **Floor** tool and create a new floor type named:
    **Steel Bar Joist 14" – Carpet on Concrete.**
    *TIP: Use a similar floor type as a starting point (duplicate) when creating new wall types.*

26. Adjust/add the layers shown in **Figure 6-6.**

FYI: Notice the Metal Deck thickness is set to 1/8" in Figure 6-6. Mtl. Deck is commonly 1 1/2", but occurs within the thickness of the concrete. If both the deck & the concrete had thickness, the floor would be shown thicker than it should be. Of course you need to consult a structural engineer to get the correct joist & slab dimensions.

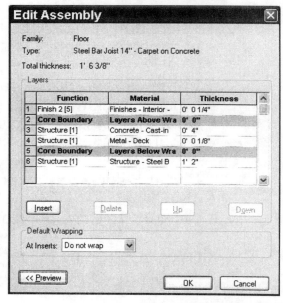

**Figure 6-6** Floor system – edit structure

Creating the second and third floors will be a little more involved than was the first floor. This is because the upper floors require several openings. For example, you need to define the openings for the elevator, the stair shafts and the atrium space. Revit makes the process very simple.

You should still be in the Floor tool.

27. In the Options Bar, check "extend into wall (to core)."

> **FYI:** The "*extend into wall (to core)*" option will extend the slab to your CMU (CMU is the core in our example), and go under the furring. Depending on the design, the floor may extend to the exterior face of the CMU, allowing the CMU to bear on the floor slab at each level. In this exercise you will select the interior side.

28. Select the exterior walls indicated in Figure 6-7. *Remember to select the interior side of the wall, use the control arrows if needed.*

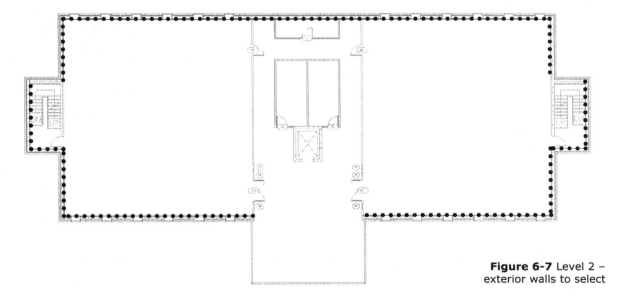

**Figure 6-7** Level 2 – exterior walls to select

Next you will define the portion of floor that extends into the stair shaft to be the landing at this level. You will need to use the line *Tool* and the *Trim* tool to define this area.

29. Click on the **Lines** tool from the *Design Bar.*

30. **Zoom In** to the west stair shaft.

31. Draw a <u>horizontal</u> line defining the edge of the landing, use Revit's snaps to accurately pick the top riser as shown in **Figure 6-8**.

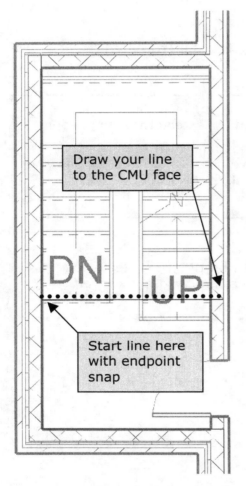

**Figure 6-8** Level 2 – west stair

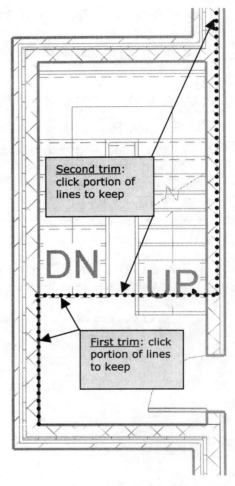

**Figure 6-9** Level 2 – west stair trim lines

32. Select the trim tool and trim the three lines referenced in **Figure 6-9**.

33. Repeat these steps for the east stair shaft.

34. Pick the four walls at the elevator shaft, select the shaft side of the wall, and then use the **Pick Walls** feature from the design bar.

You are now ready to define the edge of slab at the atrium.

35. Use the **Lines** tool to draw the edge of slab in the atrium (5 lines) as shown in **Figure 6-10**.

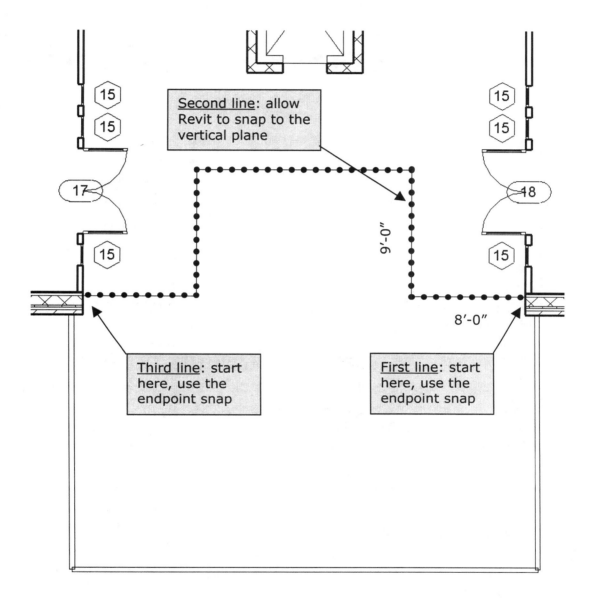

**Figure 6-10** Atrium slab definition

36. Click **Finish Sketch.**

37. Click **Yes** to the prompt "*Would you like the walls that go up to this floor's level to attach to its bottom?*"

38. Click **No** for the prompt to join the walls that overlap the floor system. (Figure 6-11)

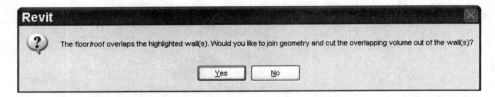

**Figure 6-11** Join walls to floor prompt

39. Change level 2's Visibility to turn off the floor hatch.

That completes the level 2 floor system. Next you will copy the floor you just created to Level 3.

40. Select the Level 2 floor you just created and select **Copy to Clipboard** from the *Edit* pull-down menu.

---

*TIP:* Selecting objects that overlap, like the exterior walls and the edge of slab (floor system), may require the use of the **TAB key**. The only way to select a floor object is by picking its edge. Revit temporarily highlights objects when you move your cursor over them. But, because the floor edge may not have an "exposed" edge to select (eg. Like we have in the atrium area), you will have to toggle through your selection options for your current cursor location. With the cursor positioned over the edge of the floor (probably with an exterior wall highlighted), press the TAB key to toggle through the available options. A tool-tip will display the objects; when you see *floor:floor-name*, click the mouse.

---

41. Switch to **Level 3.**

42. Pick **Edit → Paste Aligned → Current View.**

43. Change level 3's Visibility to turn off the floor hatch.

44. Explore your work by looking at the model in 3D.
(Figure 6-12) Notice, again, how Revit automatically applies colors and patterns to surfaces to help you (and your client) better visualize your design with minimal effort.

45. Save your project as **ex6-1.rvt.**

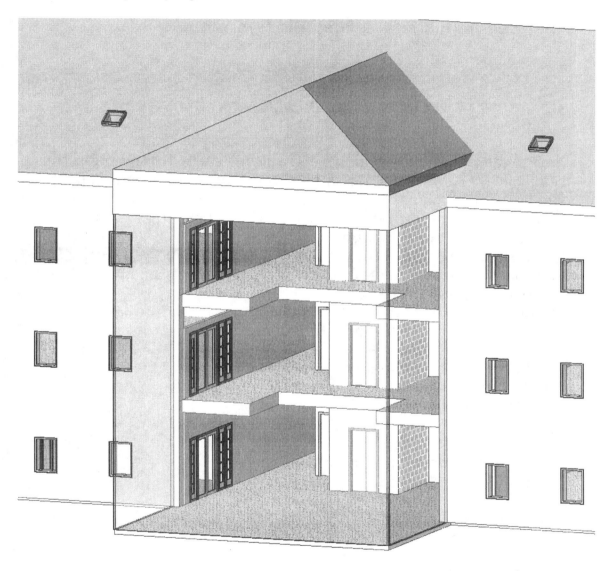

**Figure 6-12** 3D view with floors

## Exercise 6-2:
## Ceiling Systems (Susp. ACT & Gypsum Board)

This lesson will explore Revit's tools for drawing reflected ceiling plans. This will include drawing different types of ceiling systems.

### Suspended Acoustical Ceiling Tile System:

1.   Open ex6-1.rvt and Save As **ex6-2.rvt.**

2.   Switch to the **Level 1** <u>ceiling plan</u> view, from the *Project Browser.*

Notice the doors and windows are automatically turned off in the ceiling plan views. The ceiling plan views have a cutting plane similar to floor plans. You can see this setting by right-clicking on a view name in the *Project Browser* and selecting *Properties*, and then selecting **View Range**.
The default value is 7'-6".
You might increase this if, for example, you had 10'-0' ceilings and 8'-0" high doors. Otherwise, the doors would show because the 7'-6" cutting plane is below the door height.
(Figure 6-13)

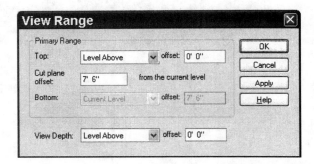

**Figure 6-13** Properties: View Range settings

3.   From the *Modeling* tab on the *Design Bar*, select **Ceiling.**

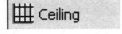

You have 5 ceiling types (by default) to select from. (Figure 6-14)

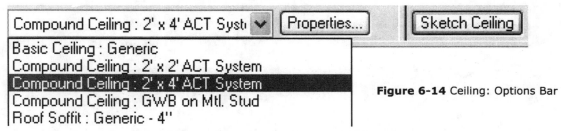

**Figure 6-14** Ceiling: Options Bar

4.   Select **Compound Ceiling: 2'x4' ACT Grid.**

Next you will change the ceiling height. The default setting is 8'-0" above the current level. You will change the ceiling height to 9'-0" to make the large open office areas feel more spacious. This setting can be changed on a room by room basis.

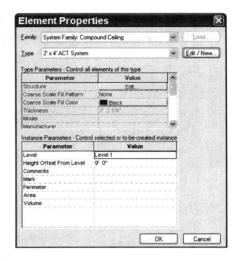

Figure 6-15 Ceiling: Properties

5.  Click the **Properties** button. (Figure 6-14)

6.  Set the *Height Offset From Level* setting to **9'-0"**. (Figure 6-15)

You are now ready to place ceiling grids. This process can not get much easier, especially compared to other CAD programs.

7.  Move your cursor anywhere within the large open office area in the west side of the building. You should see the perimeter of the room highlighted.

8.  Pick within the large room; Revit places a grid in the room. (Figure 6-16)

You now have a 2x4 ceiling grid at 9'-0" above the floor. (Level 1 in this case.)

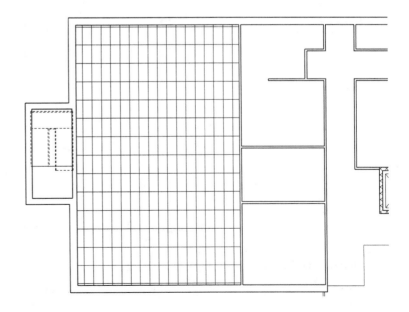

Figure 6-16 Level 1: Ceiling

When you place a ceiling grid, Revit centers the grid in the room. The general rule-of-thumb is you should try to avoid reducing the tile size by more than half at its perimeter. You can see in Figure 6-16 that the east and west sides look ok. However, the north and south sides are small slivers. You will adjust this next.

9.   Select **Modify** from the *Design Bar.*

10.  **Select** the ceiling grid (only one line will be highlighted).

11.  Use the **Move** tool to move the grid 24" to the north. (Figure 6-17)

12.  Place ceiling grids as shown in Figure 6-17.
     a.  *Be sure to adjust the ceiling heights shown in Figure 6-17.*
     b.  *Adjust the grids to avoid small tiles at the perimeter.*

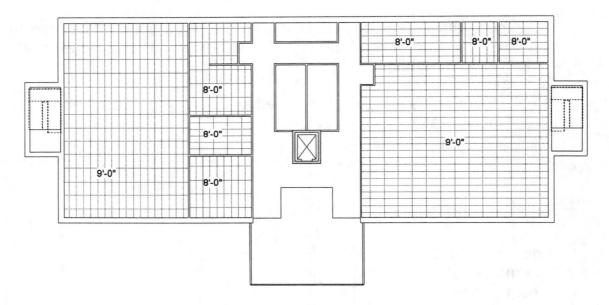

**Figure 6-17** Level 1: Ceiling Grids

## Modifying the Suspended Acoustical Ceiling Tile System:

Making modifications to the grid is relatively easy.  Next, you will adjust the ceiling height and rotate the grid.

13.  Zoom in to the room in the upper right corner on *Level 1.*

14. Select the grid and then select the **Properties** button from the *Options Bar.*

15. Change the height to **8'-6"**, then click **OK**.

16. With the grid still selected, pick **Compound Ceiling: 2'x2' ACT Grid** from the *Type Selector* on the *Options Bar.*

17. Again, with the grid still selected, use the Rotate tool to rotate the grid 45 degrees.

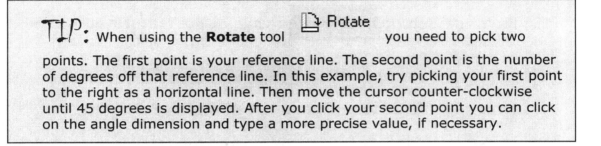

TIP: When using the **Rotate** tool ⬛ Rotate  you need to pick two points. The first point is your reference line. The second point is the number of degrees off that reference line. In this example, try picking your first point to the right as a horizontal line. Then move the cursor counter-clockwise until 45 degrees is displayed. After you click your second point you can click on the angle dimension and type a more precise value, if necessary.

18. Your drawing should look similar to **Figure 6-18**.

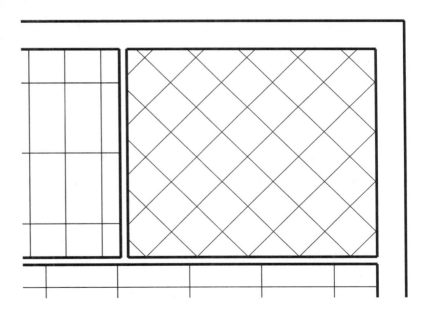

**Figure 6-18** Level 1: Modified Ceiling

Next, you will look at drawing gypsum board (or drywall) ceiling systems. The process is identical to placing the grid system. Additionally, you will create a ceiling type.

## Gypsum Board Ceiling System:

You will create a new ceiling type for a gypsum board ceiling. To better identify the areas that have a gyp. bd. ceiling, you will set the ceiling type to have a stipple pattern. This will provide a nice graphical representation for the gyp. bd. ceiling areas.

19. From the *Settings* pull-down menu, select **Materials**.
    This is the list of materials you select from when assigning a material to each layer in a wall system, etc.

20. Click **Duplicate** and enter the name:
    **Finishes - Interior - Gypsum Ceiling Board**.

21. In the *Surface Pattern* area, pick **Gypsum-Plaster** from the drop-down list, then click **OK**. (Figure 6-19)

The *Surface Pattern* setting is what will add the stipple pattern to the gyp. bd. ceiling areas. With this set to *none*, the ceiling has no pattern (like the Plain ceiling type).

Thus, if you wanted Carpet 1 finish to never have the stipple hatch pattern, you could change the surface pattern to none via the Materials dialog and not have to change each views visibility override.

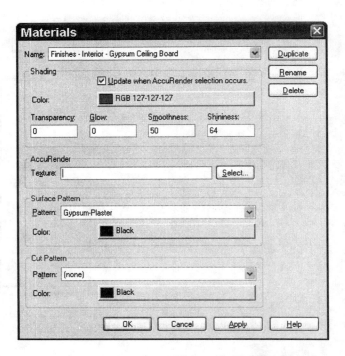

**Figure 6-19** Material dialog

22. From the *Modeling* tab on the *Design Bar*, select **Ceiling**.

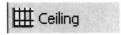

23. Click the **Properties** button. (Figure 6-14)

24. Set the Type to **GWB on Mtl. Stud**. *FYI, you are selecting this because it is similar to the ceiling you will be creating.*

25. Click the **Edit / New** button.

26. Click **Duplicate** and type **Gypsum Board** for the name.

27. Select **Edit** next to the Structure parameter.

28. Set the Values as follows: (Figure 6-20)
    a. **1 ½" Mtl. Stud**
    b. **¾" Mtl. Stud**
    c. **Finished – Interior – Gypsum Ceiling Board**
       *(This is the material you created in step 21.)*

29. Click **OK** three times.

> **FYI:** The ceiling assembly you just created represents a typical suspended gyp. bd. ceiling system. The Metal Studs are perpendicular to each other and suspended by wires, similar to an ACT (acoustical ceiling tile) system.

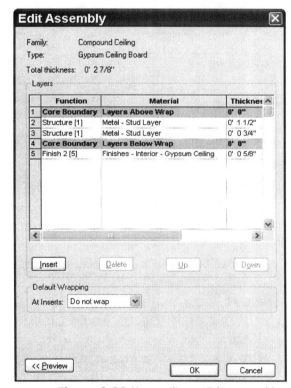

**Figure 6-20** New ceiling – Edit assembly

You are now ready to draw a gypsum board ceiling.

30. Make sure **Gypsum Board** is selected in the *Type Selector* on the *Options Bar.*

31. Set the ceiling height to **8'-0"**.

32. Pick the two bathrooms: the two rooms north of the elevator. (Figure 6-21)

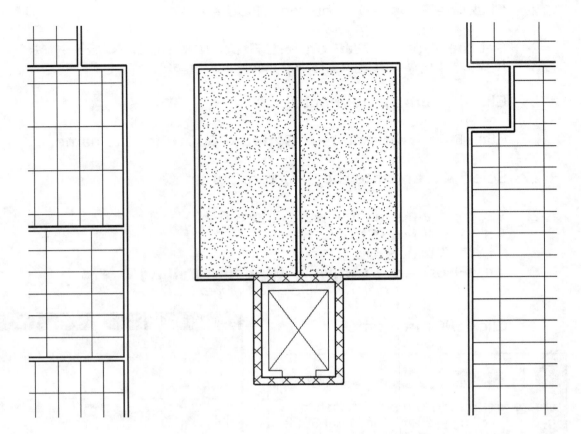

**Figure 6-21** Gyp. Bd. Ceiling

You now have a gypsum board ceiling at 8'-0" above the finished floor in the toilet rooms.

## Sketching a Ceiling:

Next, you will draw a ceiling in the atrium area. However, you cannot simply pick the room to place the ceiling because of the opening in the floor. You will need to sketch the ceiling just like you sketched the floor system in the previous exercise. First, you will need to draw a bulkhead at the edge of the second floor slab. A bulkhead is a portion of wall that hangs from the floor above and creates a closed perimeter for a ceiling system to die into.

33. While still in the Level 1 Reflected Ceiling Plan view, select the **Wall** tool.

34. Click **Properties** from the *Options Bar*.

35. Set the *wall type* to: **Interior - 4 7/8" Partition (1-hr)** and the *Base Offset* to **9'-6"**. *(This will put the bottom of the wall to 9'-6" above the current floor level, level 1 in this case.)* (Figure 6-22)

36. Set the Top Constraint to: **Up to level: Level 2.** (Figure 6-22)

*TIP: The next time you draw a wall you will have to change the Base Offset back to 0'-0" or your wall will be 9'-6" off the floor.*

37. **Draw the bulkhead**; make sure you snap to the edge of the slab. Also, make sure the wall is under the floor system, not out in the opening. (Do this by drawing the wall either from right to left or left to right depending on how you have the Loc Line set.) (Figure 6-23)

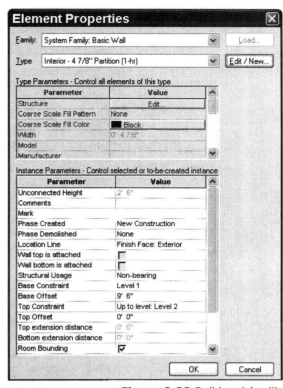

**Figure 6-22** Bulkhead (wall) properties

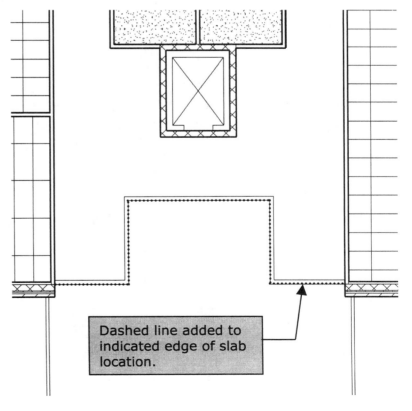

Dashed line added to indicated edge of slab location.

**Figure 6-23** Bulkhead drawn

38. Select the **Ceiling** tool and then click **Sketch Ceiling** from the *Options Bar.*

39. Use the **Pick Walls**, **Lines**, and **Trim** tools to sketch a line at the perimeter of the ceiling area as shown in **Figure 6-24**. You will also need to sketch a line around the toilet/elevator area to define the area within the larger area that will not receive the ceiling pattern: **2'x2' ACT ceiling, with the ceiling height set to 9'-6"**.

40. Click **Finish Sketch** and save Project as **ex6-2.rvt.**

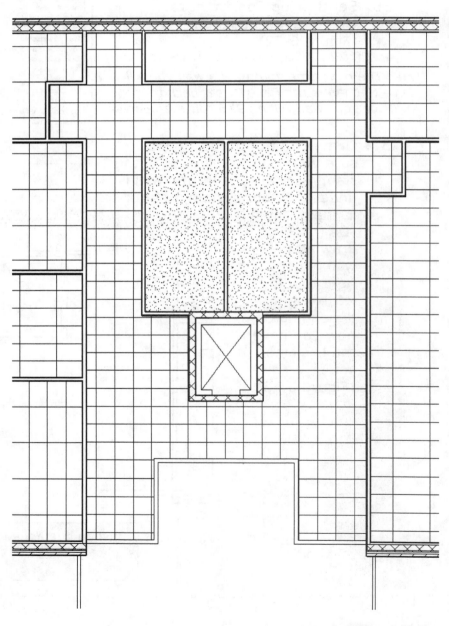

**Figure 6-24** Atrium Ceiling

## Exercise 6-3:
## Placing Fixtures (Lights and Diffusers)

In this exercise, you will learn to load and place light and mechanical fixtures in your reflected ceiling plans.

## Loading Components:

Before placing fixtures, you need to load them into your project.

1. Select **Component** from the *Modeling* tab on the *Design Bar.*

2. Select **Load from Library** on the *Options Bar.* (Figure 6-25)

**Figure 6-25** Component; Options Bar

3. Double-click the **Lighting Fixtures** folder, and then double-click **Troffer - 2x4 Parabolic.rfa**. (Figure 6-26)

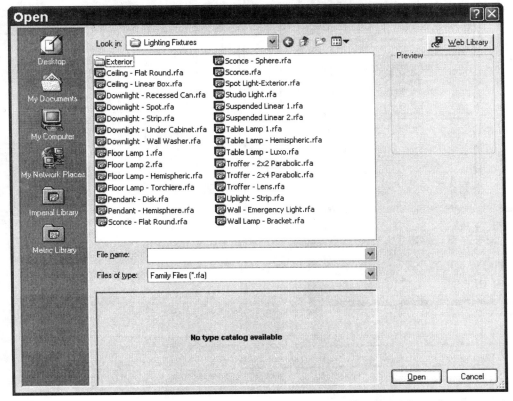

**Figure 6-26** Load component

Before placing the light fixture you will load the other fixtures first.

4. Select **Load from Library** again and then double-click on the **Mechanical Equipment** folder.

5. Select **Square Supply Diffuser** and **Square Return Register** (you can select both holding the Ctrl key) and then **Open**.

## Placing instances of components:

You are now ready to place the fixtures in your ceiling plans.

6. With **Component** still selected from the *Design Bar*, pick **Troffer – 2' x 4' Parabolic: 2'x4' (2 Lamp)** from the type selector drop down on the *Options Bar*.

7. On **Level 1 RCP**, place fixtures as shown in **Figure 6-27**.

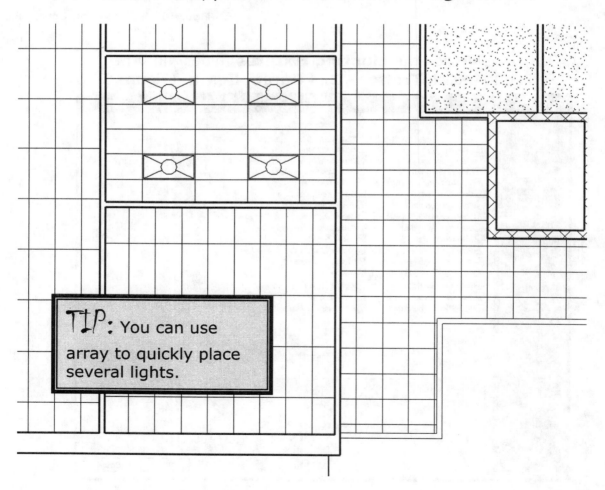

TIP: You can use array to quickly place several lights.

**Figure 6-27** RCP; lights added

You may have to use the move command to move the fixture so it fits perfectly in the ACT grid.

8. Now place a **2x4 light fixtures** as shown in **Figure 6-28**.

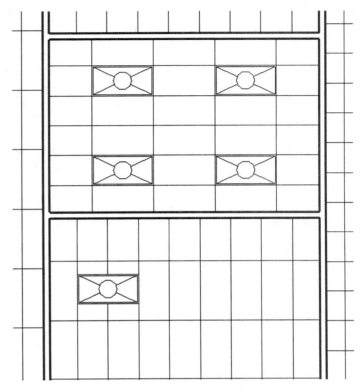

Notice the fixture does not automatically orientate itself with the ceiling grid. There may be an occasion when you want this.

Also, notice the light fixture hides a portion of the ceiling grid. This is nice because the grid does not extend through a light fixture.

**Figure 6-28** RCP; lights added

9. Use **Rotate** and **Move** to rotate the fixture to align with the grid. (Figure 6-29)

10. Once you have one fixture rotated, it is easier to use the copy tool and the snaps to add rotated light fixtures. **Copy** the light fixture to match the layout in **Figure 6-29**.

11. Select **Square Supply Diffuser: 24"x24"** from the *Type Selector*.

12. Place the diffusers as shown in Figure 6-30.

13. Select **Square Return Register: 24"x24"** from the *Type Selector*.

14. Place the Registers as shown in Figure 6-30.

15. Save your project as **ex6-3.rvt**.

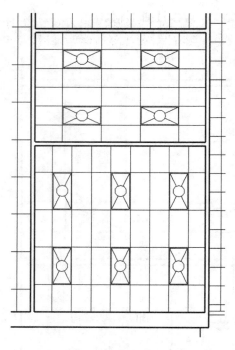

**Figure 6-29** RCP; rotated lights

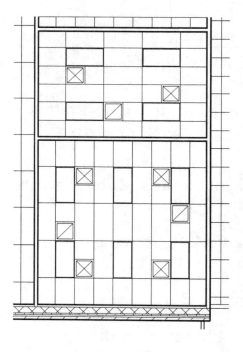

**Figure 6-30** RCP; mechanical

# Reflected Ceiling Plan Symbols:

Revit provides many of the industry standard symbols necessary in drawing reflected ceiling plans (RCP). As shown in Figure 6-28, supply air is represented with an X and return air has a diagonal line. It is typical to have a RCP symbol legend showing each symbol and material pattern and list what each one represents.

## Component Properties

If you want to adjust the properties of a component, such as a light fixture, you can browse to it in the Project Browser and right click on it *(notice the right click menu also has the option to select all instances of the item in the drawing)* and select Properties. You will see the dialog below for the 2x4 (2 Lamps).

You can also click duplicate and add more sizes (e.g. 4'x4' light fixture).

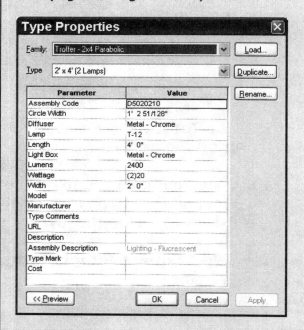

You can also select an inserted component and click the Properties button on the Options Bar for additional properties for that particular instance.

## Exercise 6-4:
## Annotations

This short section will look at adding notes to your RCP.

Adding Annotations:

1.  Select the **Text** tool from the *Design Bar.*

2.  Pick **3/32" text** from the type selector. (Figure 6-31)

3.  Select the **Leader** button circled in **Figure 6-31**.

**Figure 6-31** Text; options bar

Next, you will add a note indicating that the atrium area is open to the floor above (i.e., no floor or ceiling here). First you will draw a leader, and then Revit will allow you to type the text. To get the other leader shown in the figure below, you repeat the previous step and just enter a space for the text.

4.  Add the note "**OPEN TO ABOVE**" shown in **Figure 6-32**.

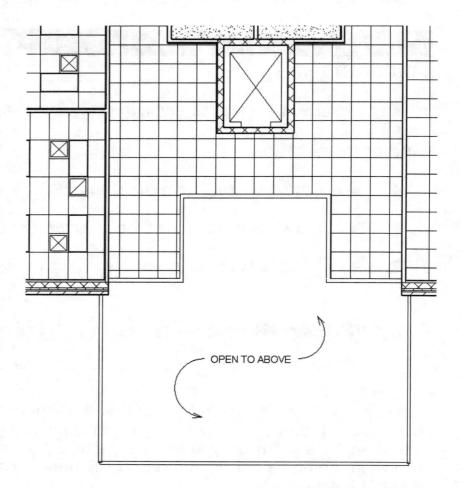

OPEN TO ABOVE

**Figure 6-32** Text with leaders

## Adding text styles to your project:

You can add additional text styles to your project. Some firms prefer a font that has a hand lettering look and others prefer Arial font. These preferences can be saved in the firms template file so they are consistent and always available. You will add a test style next.

5. Click on the **Text** tool.

6. Select **Properties** on the *Options Bar.*

7. Next, click **Edit/New**.

8.  Select **Duplicate** and enter **1/4" outline text**. (Figure 6-33)

9.  Next, make the following adjustments to the Type Properties. (Figure 6-34)
    a. Text Font: **Swis721 BdOul BT**
    b. Text Size: **1/4"**

Figure 6-33 New text name

Note: You can use any Windows true-type font. If you do not have this font, select another that best matches.

The text size you entered in step 9 is the size of the text when printed. If you change the scale of the drawing, the text size will automatically change, so the text is always the correct size when printing. It is best to set the drawing to the correct scale first. As changing the drawing scale can create a lot of work; repositioning resized text that may be overlapping something or too big for a room.

10. Select **OK** to close the dialog boxes.

You should now have the new text style available in the *Type Selector* on the *Options Bar*.

11. Use the new text style to create the text shown below. (Figure 6-35)

12. Erase the sample text (unless your instructor tells you otherwise).

13. Save as **ex6-4.rvt**.

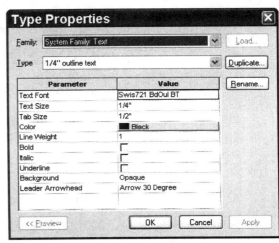

Figure 6-34 New text properties

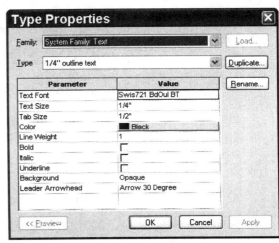

Figure 6-35 New text style sample

## Self-Exam:

The following questions can be used as a way to check your knowledge of this lesson. The answers can be found on the last page of this section.

1. You must pick Walls to define floor areas. (T/F)

2. Use the Ctrl key to cycle through the selection options. (T/F)

3. When you add a floor object in plan view, the floor does not show up right away in the other views; i.e. 3D, Sections, Etc. (T/F)

4. You use the _____ tool; if you need to add a new product, like exterior plaster, so you can add it to wall types and other systems.

5. You have _____ different types of leader options with the text tool.

## Review Questions:

The following questions may be assigned by your instructor as a way to assess your knowledge of this section. Your instructor has the answers to the review questions.

1. It is not possible to create new text styles. (T/F)

2. You can add additional diffuser sizes to the group as required. (T/F)

3. The light fixtures automatically turn to align with the ceiling grid. (T/F)

4. You can adjust the ceiling height room by room. (T/F)

5. Use the _____ button to add additional objects, for insertion, into the current project (e.q. ceiling: linear box group).

6. It is not possible to place ceiling objects in what part of a ceiling plan

   _____.

7. Use the _____ tool if the ceiling grid needs to be at an angle.

8. Use the _____ tool to adjust the ceiling grid location if a ceiling tile is less than half its normal size.

9. Use the _____ tool to adjust whether an object's surface pattern is displayed (i.e. the stipple for the gypsum board ceiling).

10. What is the current size of your project (after completing exercise 6-4)?

    _____ MB.

*Self-Exam Answers:*
**1** – F, **2** – F, **3** – F, **4** – Material, **5** – 4

# Lesson 7
# Office Building: ELEVATIONS::

This lesson will cover interior and exterior elevations. The default template you started with already has the four main exterior elevations set up for you. You will investigate how Revit generates elevations and the role the elevation tag has in that process.

## Exercise 7-1:
## Creating & Viewing Parametric Exterior Elevations

Here you will look at setting up an exterior elevation and how to control some of the various options.

## Setting up an exterior elevation:

Even though you already have the main exterior elevations set, you will go through the steps necessary to set one up. Many projects have more than four exterior elevations, so all exterior surfaces are elevated.

1. Open your project, ex6-4.rvt, and **Save As ex7-1.rvt**.

2. Switch to your **Level 1** *Floor Plan* view.

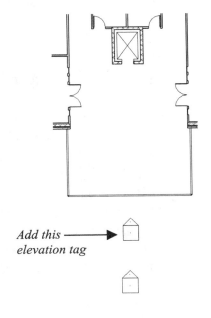

3. Select **Elevation** ⬦ Elevation , from the *View* tab on the *Design Bar*.
   *TIP: If you do not see the view tab on the Design Bar, right-click on one of the visible tabs and select View from the pop-up menu (displaying all available design bar tabs).*

4. Place the temporary elevation tag in plan view as shown in Figure 7-1.
   *Notice: As you move the cursor around the screen, the elevation tag automatically turns to point at the building.*

Add this ⟶ elevation tag

You now have an elevation added to the *Project Browser* in the *Elevations* group. This process is similar to adding another floor using the Level tool, as you did in a previous lesson.

**Figure 7-1** Added elevation tag

After placing an elevation tag, you should rename the elevation label in the project browser.

5.  In the *Project Browser*, under *Elevations*, select the elevation label that was just added.

6.  Right-click on the view label and select **Rename**.

7.  Type: **South Temp**.

The name should be fairly descriptive so you can tell where the elevation is just by the label. This will be essential on a large project that has several exterior elevations and even more interior elevations.

8.  Double-click on **South Temp** in the *Project Browser*.

The elevation may not look correct right away. You will adjust this in the next step. Notice, though, that an elevation was created simply by placing an elevation tag in plan view.

9.  Switch back to **Level 1** view.

Next you will study the options associated with the elevation tag. This, in part, controls what is seen in the elevation.

10. The elevation tag has two parts: the pointing triangle and the square center. Each part will highlight as you move the cursor over it. **Select the square center part**.

You should now see the symbol shown on the right (Figure 7-2).

**View direction boxes:**
The checked box indicates which way the elevation tag is looking. You can check (or uncheck) the other boxes.

**Rotation control:**
Allows you to look perpendicular to an angled wall in plan, for example.

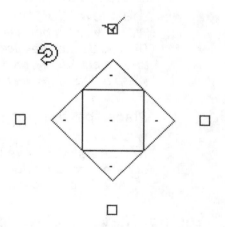

**Figure 7-2** Selected elevation tag

**Move elevation tag:**
While selected, you simply drag the tag to move it.

11. Press the **ESC** key to unselect the elevation tag.

12. Select the "pointing" portion of the elevation tag.

Your elevation tag should look similar to Figure 7-3.

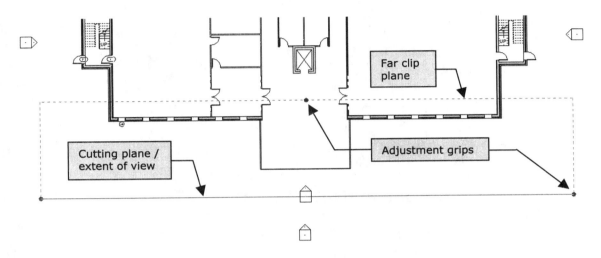

**Figure 7-3** Selected elevation tag

The elevation tag, as selected in Figure 7-3, has several features for controlling how the elevation looks. Here is a quick explanation:

- **Cutting plane/extent of view line:** This controls how much of the 3D model is elevated from left to right (i.e. the width of the elevation).
- **Far clip plane:** This controls how far into the 3D model the elevation can see.
- **Adjustment grips:** You can drag this with the mouse to control the features mention above.

13. Right-click on the view label: **South Temp** in the *Project Browser*, and then select **Properties**.

You have several options in the Properties window (Figure 7-4). Notice the three options with the check box next to them, these control the following:

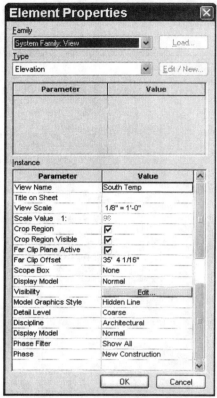

- **Crop Region**: This crops the width and height of the view in elevation. *Adjusting the width of the cropping window in elevation also adjusts the "extent of view" control in plan view.*

- **Crop Region Visible**: This displays a rectangle in the elevation view indicating the extent of the cropping window (described above). *When selected in elevation view, the rectangle can be adjusted with the adjustment grips.*

- **Far Clip Plane Active**: If this is turned off, Revit will draw everything visible in the 3D model *(within the "extent of view").*

You will manipulate some of these controls next.

**Figure 7-4** Elevation view: South Temp - Properties

14. With the elevation tag still selected (as in Figure 7-3), drag the "cutting plane/extent of view" line up into the atrium as shown in Figure 7-5.

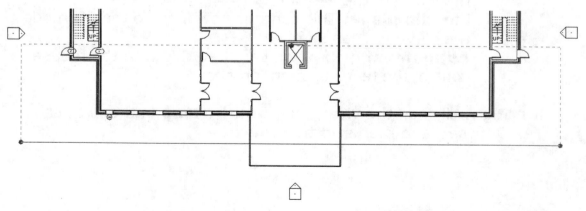

**Figure 7-5** Revised cutting plane

15. Now switch to the *Elevation view*: **South Temp**.

Your elevation should look similar to Figure 7-6. If required, click on the cropping window and resize it to match Figure 7-6.

The atrium curtain wall and roof are now displayed in section because of the location of the "cutting plane" line in plan.

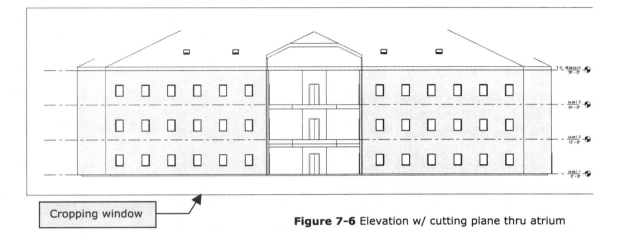

Cropping window

**Figure 7-6** Elevation w/ cutting plane thru atrium

Notice that the roof is not fully visible. This is not related to the cropping window shown in Figure 7-6. Rather, it is related to the "Far Clip Plane" set in the plan view.

16. Adjust the "Far Clip Plane" in **Level 1** plan view so that the entire roof shows in the **South Temp** view.

Next you will adjust the elevation tag to set up a detail elevation for the atrium curtain wall.

17. In **Level 1** plan view, adjust the elevation tag to show only the atrium curtain wall (Figure 7-7).

18. Switch to **South Temp** view to see the "detail" elevation (Figure 7-8).

19. Adjust the South Temp view's Properties to turn off the crop window's visibility.

20. **Save** your project as **ex7-1.rvt**.

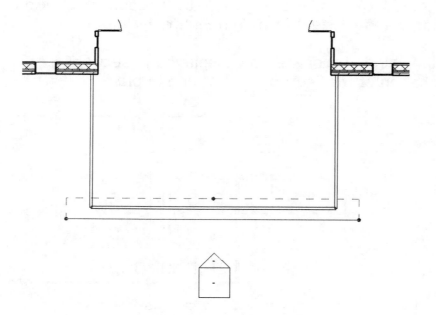

**Figure 7-7** Atrium curtain wall detail elevation

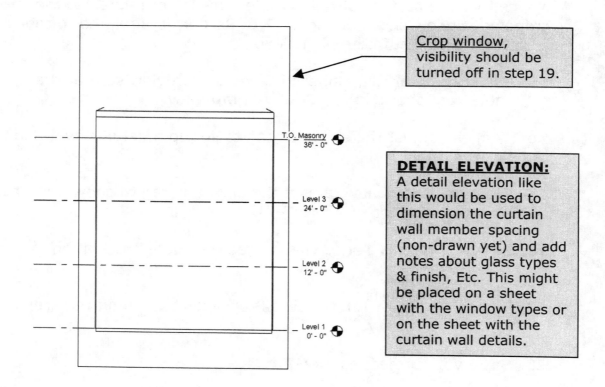

Crop window, visibility should be turned off in step 19.

T.O. Masonry
36' - 0"

Level 3
24' - 0"

Level 2
12' - 0"

Level 1
0' - 0"

**DETAIL ELEVATION:**
A detail elevation like this would be used to dimension the curtain wall member spacing (non-drawn yet) and add notes about glass types & finish, Etc. This might be placed on a sheet with the window types or on the sheet with the curtain wall details.

**Figure 7-8** Atrium curtain wall detail elevation

## Exercise 7-2:
## Modifying the Project Model: Exterior Elevations

The purpose of this exercise is to demonstrate that changes can be made anywhere and all other drawings are automatically updated.

### Modify an exterior elevation:

1.  Open ex7-1.rvt and **Save As ex7-2**.

2.  Open the **East** exterior elevation view.

3.  Use the Window tool and select **Fixed: 32" x 48"**.

You will insert a window in elevation. This will demonstrate, first, that you can actually add a window in elevation not just plan view, and second, that the other views are automatically updated.

Notice, with the window selected for placement, you have the usual dimensions helping you accurately place the window. As you move the window around you should see a dashed horizontal green line indicating the default sill height.

4.  Place a window as shown in **Figure 7-9**.

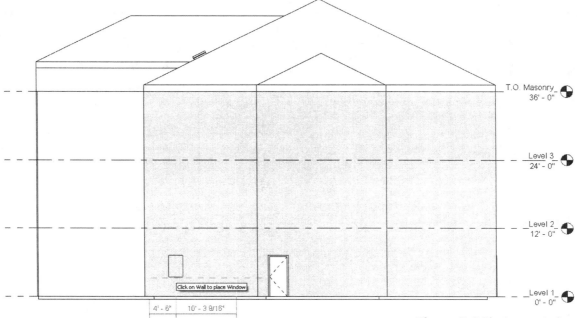

**Figure 7-9** Placing a window

5.   Switch to **Level 1** plan view; notice the window is added.
     (Figure 7-10)

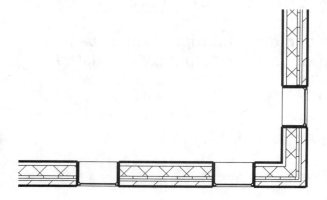

TIP: If the window is towards the inside, use the control arrows to flip the window within the wall. It should look like the window in Figure 7-10.

**Figure 7-10** Level 1 – south-east corner

6.   Switch back to the **East** elevation view.

7.   Add windows as shown in Figure 7-11 (*on next page*).

If you laid out the interior walls as described in lesson 3, you should get a warning message when inserting the windows on level 1, towards the north side of the building. This is because the interior wall for the room in the north-east corner conflicts with the exterior window. Revit is smart enough to see that conflict and bring it to your attention. In this case you probably want the windows to be uniformly spaced, so you will Ignore the conflict and move the wall in plan view.

8.   Click Ignore for the wall / Window conflict warning
     (Figure 7-12). *If you did not get this warning, skip this step.*

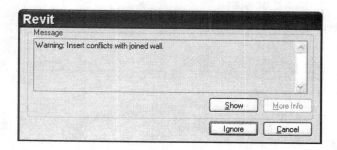

**Figure 7-12** Conflict warning

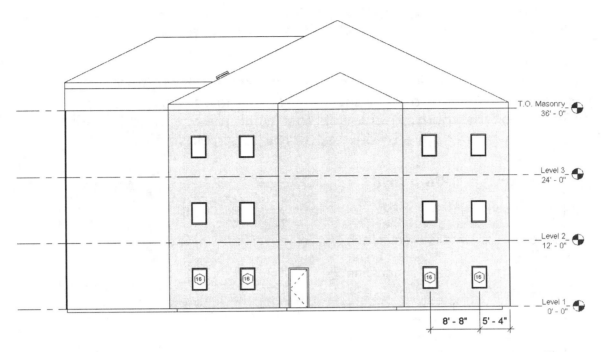

**Figure 7-11** East elevation
– windows added

9.   Switch to **Level 1** plan view and revise the wall as shown in **Figure 7-13**. *TIP: You will need to use the split tool to break the wall where it offsets. You can then select the wall (just the wall, the doors will automatically move with the wall) and use the Move tool to move it north. Also notice that the windows on the east wall need to be flipped.*

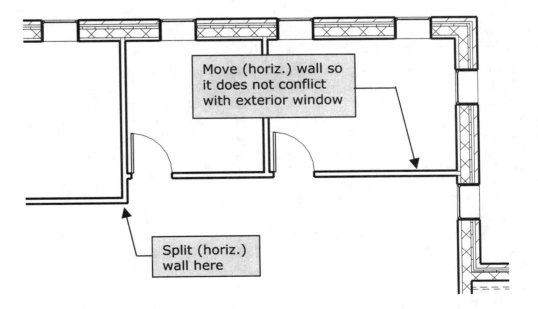

**Figure 7-13** Level 1 – north-east corner

10. Switch to the **Level 1** RCP view. *Notice the ceiling grids are likely not aligned with the revised walls. If this is the case, see the explanation below (Figure 7-14).*

Most of the time, when you move a wall, Revit will automatically update the ceiling gird to fit the new room. However, occasionally the definition of the room boundary is lost while making modifications. In this case, you will have to delete the grid and reinsert it.

**Deleting a ceiling grid:**

When selecting a ceiling grid, Revit only selects one line. This does not allow you to delete the ceiling grid. To delete: hover cursor over a ceiling grid line and press the TAB key until you see the ceiling perimeter highlight, then click the mouse. The entire ceiling will be selected. Press Delete.

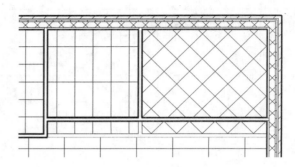

**Figure 7-14** Level 1 RCP – north-east corner

11. Add the same layout of windows (Figure 7-11), to the west elevation. *Tip: mirror the windows in plan view, each floor*

12. **Save** your Project as ex7-2.rvt.

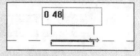

𝒯𝐼𝑃: ENTERING DIMENSIONS IN REVIT

As your experience with Revit grows, you will want to learn some of the shortcuts to using the program. One of those short cuts is how you enter dimensions when drawing. You probably already know, maybe by accident, that if you enter only one number (e.g., 48) and press enter, Revit interprets that number to be feet (e.g., 48'-0"). So, if you want to enter 48", you may be typing 0'-48" or 48". Both work, but having to press the shift key to get the inch symbol takes a little longer.

Here are some options for entering dimensions:

**0 48**     *Revit reads this as 48"* (zero space forty-eight)
**48**        *Revit reads this as 48'-0"*
**5.5**       *Revit reads this as 5'-6"*
**0 5.5**    *Revit reads this as 5 ½"*
**2 0 1/4**  *Revit reads this as 2'-0 ¼"* (two space zero space fraction)

## Exercise 7-3:
## Creating & Viewing Parametric Interior Elevations

Creating interior elevations is very much like exterior elevations. In fact, you use the same tool. The main difference is that you are placing the elevation tag inside the building, rather than on the exterior.

## Adding interior elevation tag:

1.   Open project ex7-2.rvt and **Save As ex7-3.rvt**.

2.   Switch to **Level 1** floor plan view, if necessary.

3.   Select the **Elevation** tool. 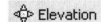 Elevation

4.   Place an elevation tag, looking east, in the atrium area. (Figure 7-15)

**Remember**, the first thing you should do after adding an elevation tag is to give it an appropriate name in the *Project Browser* list.

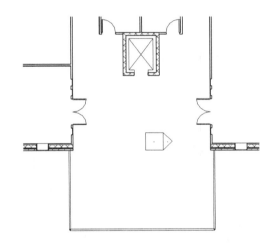

5.   Change the name of the elevation to **East Atrium**.

6.   Switch to the East Atrium view. *Try double-clicking on the elevation tag.*

**Figure 7-15** Level 1 - Atrium

Initially, your elevation should look something like Figure 7-16. You will adjust this view next. *Notice how Revit automatically controls the lineweights of things in section vs. things in elevations.*

> **FYI:** the elevation tags are used to reference the sheet and drawing number so the client or contractor can find the desired elevation quickly while looking at the floor plans. This will be covered in a later lesson. It is interesting to know, however, that Revit automatically does this (fills in the elevation tag) when the elevation is placed on a sheet, and will update it if the elevation is moved.

7.   Switch back to the
     **Level 1** view.

8.   Pick the "pointing"
     portion of the elevation
     tag, so you see the view
     options. (Figure 7-17)

You should compare the two
drawings on this page (Figures
7-16 & 7-17) to see how the
control lines in the plan view
dictate what is generated/
visible in the elevation view,
for both width and depth.

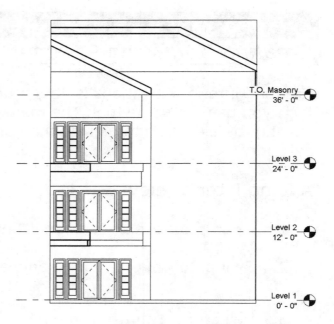

**Figure 7-16** East Atrium – initial view

The goal is to set up an interior elevation of the entire east atrium
wall, with the floor structure and roof shown in section.

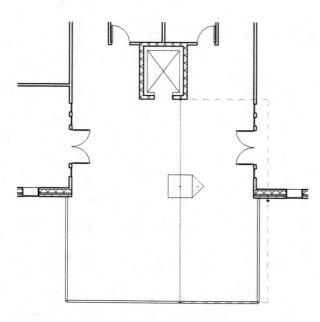

**Figure 7-17** Elevation tag selected

9. Adjust the control lines for the elevation tag as shown in Figure 7-18. Drag the "cutting plane/extent of view" line to the location shown. Make sure the "far clip plane" extends past the door alcove; otherwise it will not show up.

10. Switch back to the **East Atrium** view.

Other than adjusting the height of the view, you have the view ready.

11. Select the cropping window and drag the top middle grip upward, to increase the view size vertically. (Figure 7-19)

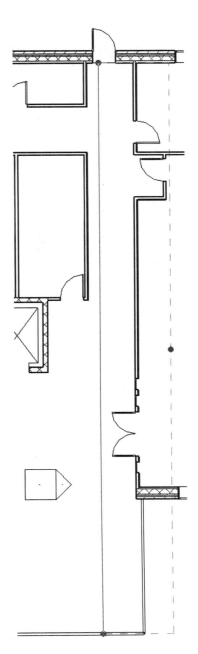

Top middle grip

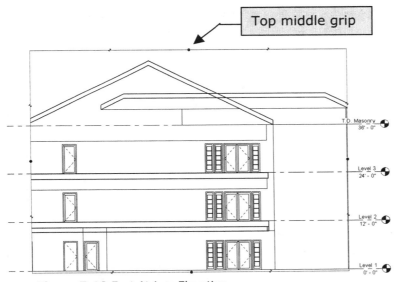

**Figure 7-19** East Atrium Elevation – crop window selected

**Figure 7-18** Elevation tag adjustments

If the ceiling were drawn for the third floor (your instructor may have assigned this), you would probably stretch the crop window down to it. Interior elevations don't normally show walls, roofs & floors in section. An atrium elevation like this could be an exception for the floors.

12. Now stretch the top of the crop window down to approximately 9'-6" above level 3 (go to the ceiling if you have drawn one for level 3).

13. Stretch the bottom of the crop window up to align with the top of the level 1 floor slab.

14. In the view **Properties**, set the scale to **1/4"=1'-0"**.

Your elevation should look like Figure 7-20.

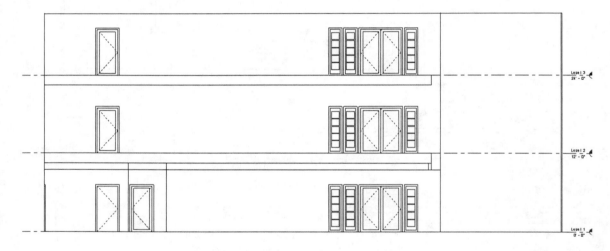

**Figure 7-20** East Atrium Elevation

You can leave the crop window on to help define the perimeter of the elevation. You can also turn it off. However, some lines that are directly under the crop window might disappear. You could use the Line tool to manually define the perimeter.

Also, notice the level tag automatically resized to match the new scale. When space permits, most interior elevations are 1/4" = 1'-0".

15. Save your project as **ex7-3.rvt**.

## Exercise 7-4:
## Modifying the Project Model: Interior Elevations

This short exercise, similar to exercise 7-2, will look at an example of Revit's parametric change engine. All drawings are generated from one 3D model.

Modify the interior elevations:

1. Open ex7-3.rvt and **Save As ex7-4.rvt**.

2. Open the **East Atrium** elevation view.

You will move two doors and add one.

3. Select both of the single doors on levels 2 and 3; use the Ctrl key to select multiple objects at one time.

4. Use the **Move** tool to move the door 6'-0" to the right (south). (Figure 7-21)

5. In the East Atrium elevation view, use the door tool to place a **Sgl Flush: 36" x 84"** door on Level 2 to the far left (north). (Figure 7-21)

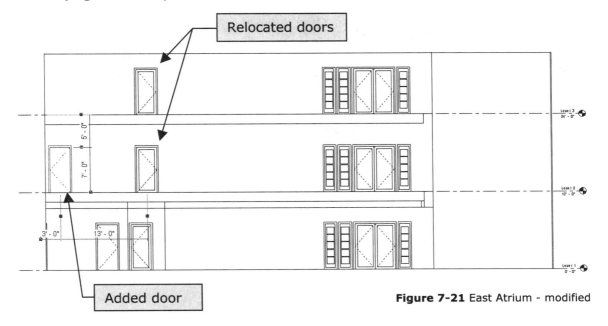

**Figure 7-21** East Atrium - modified

Now it's time to see the effects to the plan views.

6. Switch to **Level 2** floor plan view. (Figure 7-22)
   *You can also see a similar change on Level 3.*

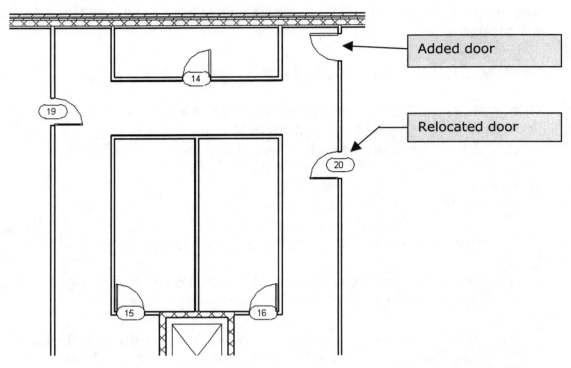

**Figure 7-22** Level 2 plan w/ changes

In elevation, you can adjust many things this way. Some examples are: ceiling height, interior and exterior windows, wall locations (perpendicular to the current view), etc.

7. Save your project as **ex7-4.**

## Exercise 7-5:
## Adding Mullions to a Curtainwall

This exercise will cover the steps involved in designing a curtainwall system (only from an aesthetic viewpoint, not structurally). This is surprisingly simple to do.

## Adding Curtain Grid:

First, you draw a grid on your curtainwall. This sets up the location for your mullions, which you will add later.

1. Open ex7-4.rvt and **Save As ex7-5.rvt**.

2. Switch to your **South Temp** view.

3. From the *Modeling* tab on the *Design Bar*, select **Curtain Grid**.

4. Draw the grid as shown in **Figure 7-23**.
   *Be sure to add horizontal grids the levels 2 and 3.*

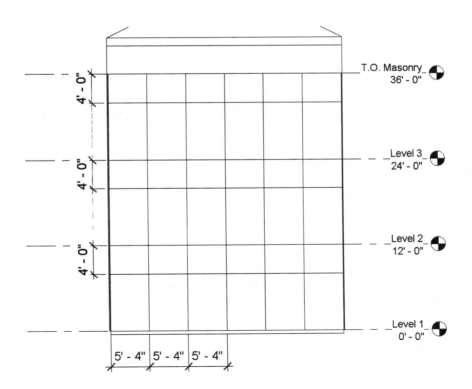

**Figure 7-23** South Temp view – curtain grid added

If a curtain grid line did not land in the correct place, you can select it and adjust the dimensions that will appear on the screen. To select the grid you need to place your cursor over the grid line and press the Tab key until the curtain grid is highlighted, and then click to select.

5.   Select the *Curtain Grid* tool and then click on the **One Segment** option on the *Options Bar.* (Figure 7-24)

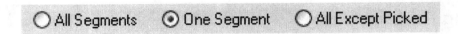

O All Segments    ⊙ One Segment    O All Except Picked

**Figure 7-24** Options Bar for Curtain Grid tool

6.   Draw two vertical lines to set up the main entry door location. (Figure 7-25)   *You do not need to draw the dimensions shown.*

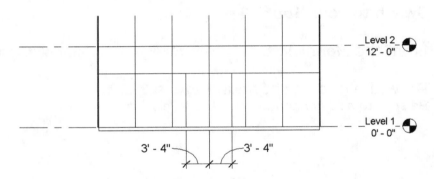

**Figure 7-25** Curtain grid for door location

Notice that the One Segment option limits the grid to the "cell" you clicked in, rather than extending from top to bottom as the others did.

Next, you will set up the curtain grid lines around the corners. This can be done from the east or west views, similar to the previous steps. However, this can also be accomplished in a 3D view.

7.   Click on the **3D** icon on the *View* toolbar.

8.   Using the Curtain Grid tool, add the grid lines shown in **Figure 7-26**. Starting at the outside corner, space the grids 5'-4" (the last space will be smaller).

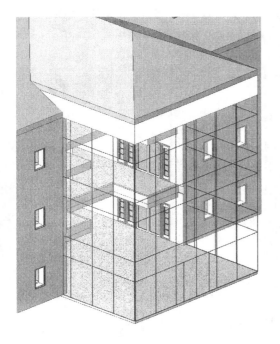

As you move the cursor, while placing the horizontal grids, you should see the grid "snap" to the grid around the corner; that is when you click the mouse.

Use the Dynamically Modify View tool to see your project from different views.

**Figure 7-26** Curtain grid – 3D view

## Adding Doors:

9.  Switch back to South Temp view and select one of the 3'-4" wide cells; place your cursor over the cell and press the Tab key until that cell is highlighted and then click to select.

10. With the cell selected, pick **Curtain Wall Sgl Glass** from the *Type Selector* on the *Options Bar*. (Figure 7-27)  *If that type is not loaded, click on Properties and then Load. Load the style from the Doors folder.*

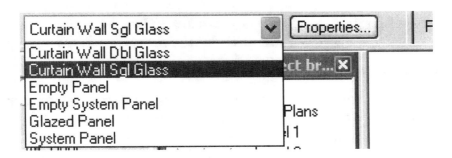

**Figure 7-27** Type selector with curtain wall cell selected

11. Repeat the previous two steps for the other 3'-4" wide cell. (Figure 7-28)

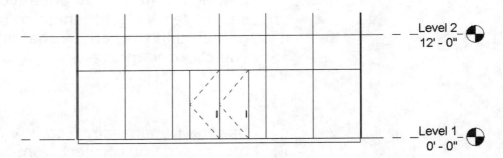

_Level 2_
12' - 0"

_Level 1_
0' - 0"

**Figure 7-28** Curtain grid with doors added

## Adding Curtainwall Mullions:

Thus far you have simply setup the spacing for the curtainwall mullions. Next you need to place the curtainwall mullions. This involves selecting a size for the mullion, as they typically come in many shapes and sizes (the depth is usually related to the height of the curtainwall, as the mullion acts as the structure for the glass wall).

12. Switch to the **3D** view.

13. Select the **Mullion** tool from the *Modeling tab.*

14. Select **Rectangular Mullion – 2.5" x 5" rectangular** from the type selector. (Figure 7-29)

**Figure 7-29** Type selector for Mullion tool

15. Select all the grid lines you previously placed and the perimeter (excluding the outside corners and the bottom horizontal member on the south face).

Next, you will add the horizontal mullion at the bottom, on the south side. You need to place this mullion so it does not extend through the door openings.

16. With the Mullion tool selected, click **Grid Line Segment** from the *Options Bar.* (Figure 7-29)

17. Click on the bottom edge of the six cells (skipping the two door openings), to place the horizontal mullion. (Figure 7-30)

**Figure 7-30** 3D view with mullions added

In this example, you will not place a corner mullion. This will be a butt-joint condition where the two panes of glass are held together with silicon in the corner.

All views will now be updated to show the curtainwall mullions.

18. Switch to the **Level 1** plan view to see the added curtainwall mullions and doors. (Figure 7-31)

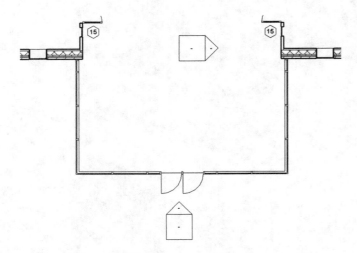

**Figure 7-31** Level 1 plan view with curtainwall mullions

19. **Save** your project as **ex7-5.rvt**.

## Self-Exam:

The following questions can be used as a way to check your knowledge of this lesson. The answers can be found on the last page of this section.

1. The plan is updated automatically when an elevation is modified, but not the other way around. (T/F)

2. You can use the Elevation tool to place both interior and exterior elevations. (T/F)

3. You can rename elevation views to better manage them. (T/F)

4. You have to resize the level tags and annotations after changing a view's scale. (T/F)

5. How do you enter 5 ½" without entering the foot or inch symbol?

_____

## Review Questions:

The following questions may be assigned by your instructor as a way to assess your knowledge of this section. Your instructor has the answers to the review questions.

1. The visibility of the crop window can be controlled. (T/F)

2. You have to manually adjust the lineweights in the elevations. (T/F)

3. As you move the cursor around the building, during placement, the elevation tag turns to point at the building. (T/F)

4. There is only one part of the elevation tag that can be selected. (T/F)

5. You cannot adjust the "extent of view" (width) using the crop window. (T/F)

6. What is the first thing you should do after placing an elevation tag?

_____

7. In addition to the Window tool, if one window is already placed, you can use the _____ tool to place additional instances of that window.

8. With the elevation tag selected, you can use the _____ to adjust the tag orientation to look at an angled wall.

9. You need to adjust the _____ to see objects, in elevation, that are a distance back from the main elevation.

10. _____ don't normally show walls/roofs/floors in section.

*Self-Exam Answers:*
**1** – F, **2** – T, **3** – T, **4** – F, **5** – 0 5.5

**Notes:**

# Lesson 8
# Office Building: SECTIONS::

Sections are one of the main communication tools in a set of architectural drawings. They help the builder understand vertical relationships. Architectural sections can occasionally contradict other drawings, such as mechanical or structural drawings. One example is a beam shown on the section is smaller than what structural shows; this creates a problem in the field when the duct does not fit in the ceiling space. The ceiling gets lowered and/or the duct gets smaller, ultimately compromising the design to a certain degree.

Revit takes great steps toward eliminating these types of conflicts. Sections, like plans and elevations, are generated from the 3D model. So it is virtually impossible to have a conflict between the architectural drawings. The final step will be to get the engineers working on the same 3D model; this would eliminate conflicts and redundancy in drawing.

## Exercise 8-1:
## Specify section cutting plane in plan view

Similar to elevation tags, placing the reference tags in a plan view actually generates the section view. You will learn how to do this next.

Placing section tags:

1. Open ex7-5.rvt and **Save As ex8-1.rvt**.

2. Switch to **Level 1** view.

3. Select the **Section** tool from the **Basics** tab on the *Design Bar*.          ⬧ Section

4. Draw a Section tag as shown in Figure 8-1. Start on the left side in this case. Use the Move tool if needed to accurately adjust the section tag after insertion. The section should go through the doors in the stair shaft. (Figure 8-1)

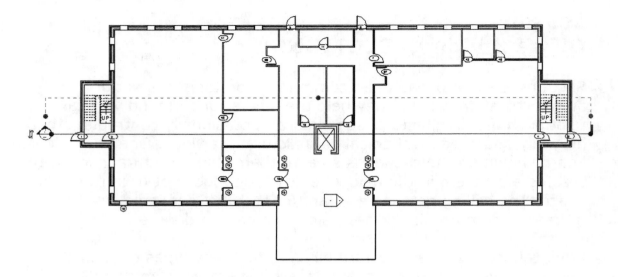

**Figure 8-1** Section tag (selected)

Figure 8-1 shows the section tag selected. The section tag features are very similar to the elevation tags covered in the previous lesson. You can adjust the depth of view (far clip plane) and the width of the section with the *Adjustment Grips*.

Section views are listed under that heading in the *Project Browser*. Similar to newly created elevation views, you should name section views as you create them.

5.  Rename the new section view to: **Longitudinal Section**.

6.  Switch to the **Longitudinal Section** view. (Figure 8-2)

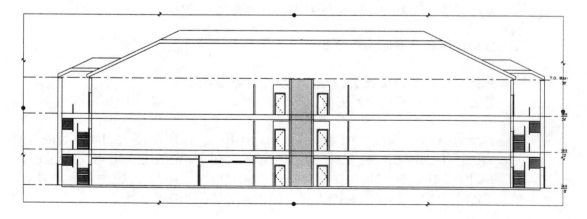

**Figure 8-2** Longitudinal section view

You can see that the stairs are cut off on the back side because of the *Far Clip Plane* location in the plan view. Also, you can see the roof is shown in section exactly where the section line is shown in plan. Figure 8-2 also shows the *Crop Region*.

7.  Adjust the Far Clip Plane in plan view so all the stair shows and the Crop Region is not visible. (Figure 8-3)

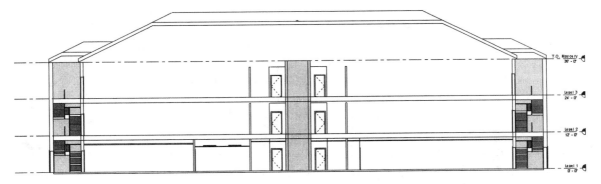

**Figure 8-3** Longitudinal view - updated

8.  Change the view *Properties* so the **Detail Level** is set to **Medium**.

9.  Switch back to the section and zoom in to the elevator shaft area as shown in **Figure 8-4**.

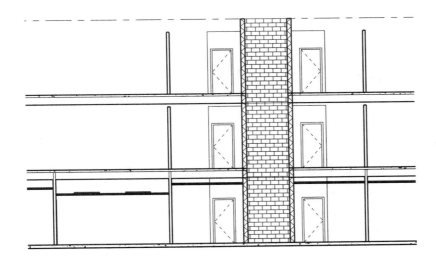

**Figure 8-4** Section view – zoomed in

You should notice an added level of detail in the section view. For example, the concrete hatch in the floor and the CMU joint lines in the elevator shaft. This added detail helps the drawing read better.

Next you will add a cross sectional view.

10. Create a **Section** as shown in **Figure 8-5**.
    *TIP: you can use the control arrows to make the section look the other direction.*

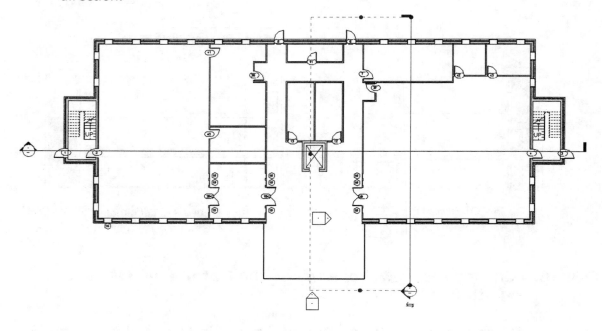

**Figure 8-5** Level 1 view; Section tag (selected)

11. Rename the new section view to **Cross Section 1** in the *Project Browser*.

12. Adjust the **Far Clip Plane** so the entire atrium roof will be visible in the **Cross Section 1** view.

13. Switch to the **Cross Section 1** view.

14. Set the *Detail Level* to **Medium** and turn off the **Crop Region** visibility in the View Properties. (Figure 8-6)

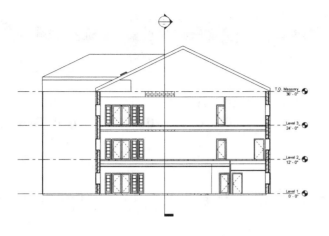

**Figure 8-6** Cross Section 1 view

Revit automatically displays lines heavier for objects that are in section than for objects beyond the cutting plane and shown in elevation.

Also, with the Detail Level set to medium, the walls and floors are hatched to represent the material in section.

Notice that the Longitudinal Section tag is automatically displayed in the Cross Section 1 view. If you switch to the Longitudinal Section view you will see the Cross Section 1 tag. Keeping with Revit's philosophy of change anything anywhere, you can select the section tag in the other section view and adjust its various properties, like the Far Clip Plane.

15. **Save** your project as **ex8-1.rvt**.

FYI: In any view that has a Section Tag in it, you can double-click on the round reference bubble to quickly switch to that section view.

## Exercise 8-2:
## Modifying the project model in section view

Again, similar to elevation views, you can modify the project model in section view. This includes adjusting door locations and ceiling heights.

### Modifying doors in section view:

In this section you will move a door and delete a door in section view.

1. Open ex8-1.rvt and **Save As ex8-2.rvt**.

2. Open **Cross Section 1** view.

3. On **Level 2**, move the *Single Glass* door **5'-0"** to the north and **delete** the door added in a previous lesson, see modified section view Figure 8-7. (See Figure 8-6 for unmodified view.)

4. Adjust the **ceiling height** in the lower right room to be **9'-0"** above level 1. (Figure 8-7) *TIP: select the ceiling and simply change the temporary dimension that appears.*

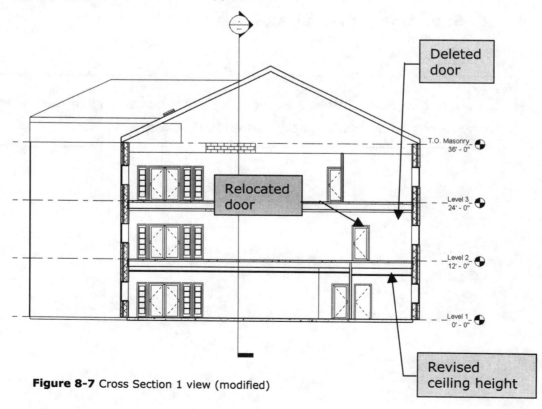

**Figure 8-7** Cross Section 1 view (modified)

5. Switch to the **Level 2** view. (Figure 8-8)

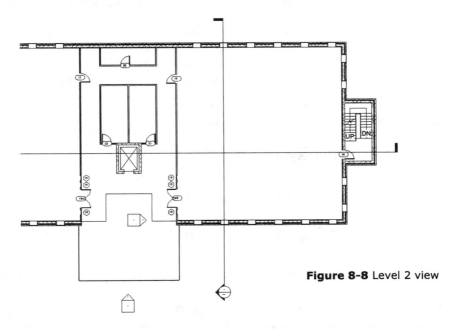

**Figure 8-8** Level 2 view

You should see the door in its new location and the other door has been deleted.

6. Switch to the **East Atrium** view (Figure 8-9)

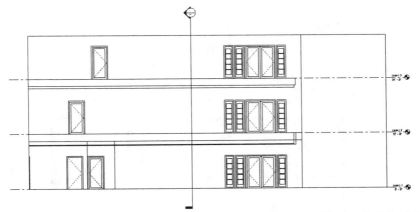

**Figure 8-9** East Atrium view

You can see the changes here as well. Compare this elevation with Figure 7-21 from lesson 7. Also, notice that the section mark was automatically added the elevation. Remember, you can double-click on the section bubble to switch to that view.

7. Save your project as **ex8-2.rvt**.

## Exercise 8-3:
## Wall Sections

So far in this lesson you have drawn building sections. Building sections are typically 1/16" or 1/8" scale and light on the detail and notes. Wall sections are drawn at a larger scale and have much more detail. You will look at setting up wall sections next.

### Setting up the Wall Section view:

1.   Open ex8-2 and **Save As ex8-3.rvt**.

2.   Switch to the **Cross Section 1** view.

3.   From the *View* tab on the *Design Bar*, select the **Callout** tool.

4.   Place a **Callout** tag as shown in Figure 8-10. *TIP: pick in the upper left and then in the lower right (don't drag) to place the Callout tag.*

5.   Use the *Control Grips* for the *Callout* tag to move the reference bubble as shown in Figure 8-10.

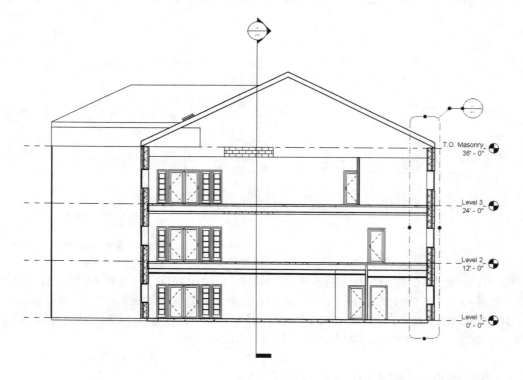

**Figure 8-10** Cross Section 1 view with Callout added

Notice that a view was added in the Sections category of the Project Browser. Because Callouts are detail references off of a section view, it is a good idea to keep the section view name similar to the name of the callout.

Additionally, Callouts differ from section views in that the callout is not referenced in every related view. This example is typical, in that the building sections are referenced from the plans and wall sections are referenced from the building sections. The floor plans can get pretty messy if you try to add too much information to them.

6. Double-click on the reference bubble portion of the Callout tag to open the **Callout of Cross Section 1** view. (Figure 8-11)

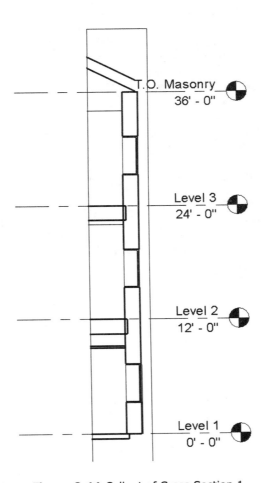

**Figure 8-11** Callout of Cross Section 1

7.  In the View properties, set the *View Scale* to **¾" = 1'-0"** and the *Detail Level* to **Fine**. (Figure 8-12)

Notice the Level tags size changed as well as the detail level. (Fig 8-13)

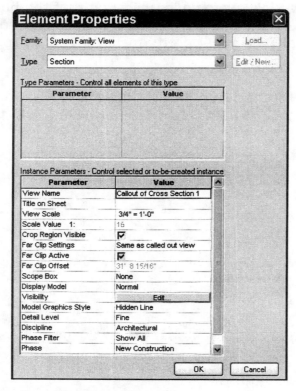

**Figure 8-12** View properties

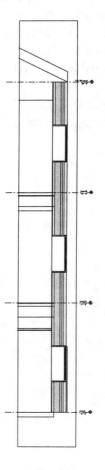

**Figure 8-13** Revised detail level & view scale

If you zoom in on a portion of the Callout view, you can see the detail added to the view. The wall interior lines are added and the materials in section are hatched.
(Figure 8-14)

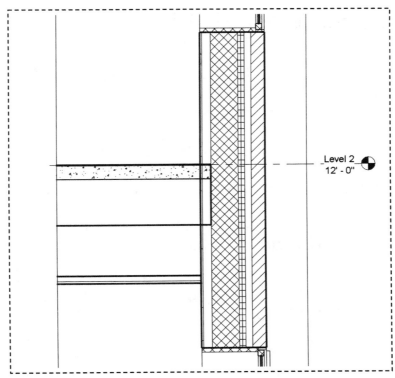

**Figure 8-14** Callout view (zoomed in)

You can use the Lines tool to add more detailed information to the drawing. For example, you could show the masonry coursing, window trim, brick vents/weeps and flashing.

As before, you can turn off and adjust the crop region.

8.   **Save** your project as **ex8-3.rvt**.

## Exercise 8-4:
## Annotation

This exercise will explore adding notes and dimensions to your wall section.

### Add notes & dimensions to Callout of Cross Section 1:

1.  Open ex8-3.rvt and **Save As ex8-4.rvt**.

2.  Switch to **Callout of Cross Section 1** view.

3.  Adjust the view properties so the crop region is not visible.

4.  Add two dimensions and adjust the Level tag location as show in **Figure 8-15**.  *TIP: dimension to the masonry opening*

These dimensions are primarily for the masons laying up the CMU & Brick. Typically, when an opening is dimensioned in masonry, the dimension has the suffix M.O. This stands for Masonry Opening, clearly representing that the dimension identifies an opening in the wall. You will add the suffix next.

5.  Select the dimension at the window opening and pick the **Properties** button from the Options Bar.

6.  Type **M.O.** in the Suffix field. (Figure 8-16)

7.  Click **OK**.

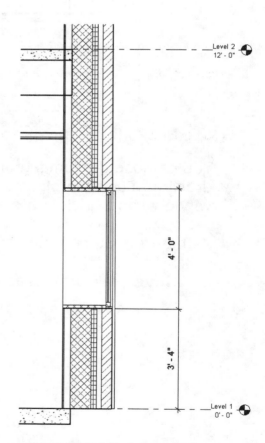

**Figure 8-15** Added dimensions

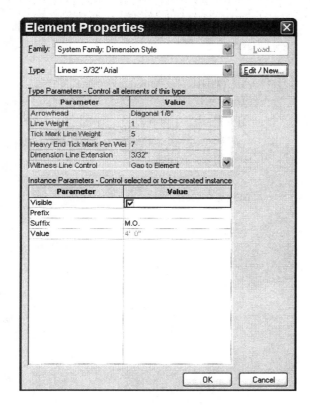

**Figure 8-16** Selected dimension properties

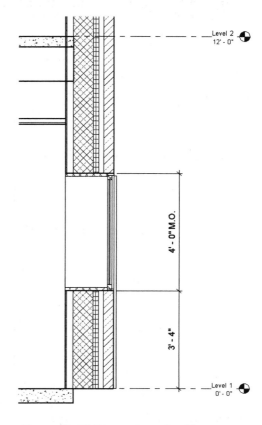

**Figure 8-17** Dimension w/ suffix

**Figure 8-17** shows the dimension with the added suffix.

8.  Add the additional dimensions shown in **Figure 8-18**; be sure to add the suffixes.

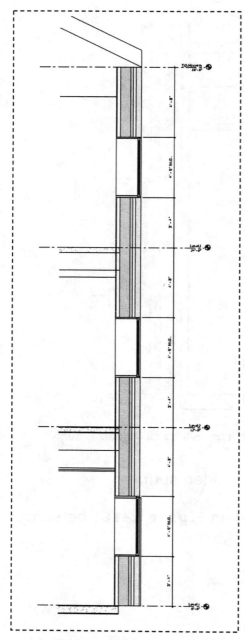

**Figure 8-18** All dimensions added

9.  Add the notes with leaders shown in Figure 8-19.

    a.  Aluminum window system, typical
    b.  Brick cavity wall
    c.  Concrete & metal deck and stl. bar joists
    d.  Concrete slab on grade over vapor barrier

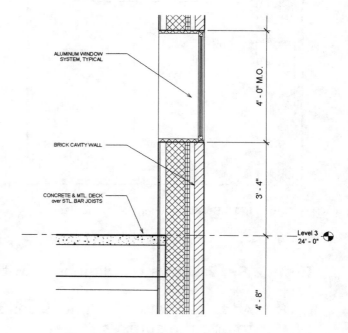

**Figure 8-19** Notes added

10. The text style should be set to **3/32" Arial**; it may still be set to the last text style you used (1/4" Outline Text, in this book).

11. Select the text and use the grips & the justification buttons to make the text look like **Figure 8-19**.

12. Save your project as **8-4.rvt**.

---

FYI: Architectural text is typically all uppercase.

---

## Self-Exam:
The following questions can be used as a way to check your knowledge of this lesson. The answers can be found on the last page of this section.

1. The controls for the section mark (when selected) are similar to the controls for the elevation mark. (T/F)

2. In large-scale elevations (and areas elevated within a section), Revit displays the masonry coursing. (T/F)

3. In large-scale sections (i.e. wall sections), Revit displays the masonry coursing in addition to the material hatching. (T/F)

4. The "Crop Region" is represented by a red line in the section view. (T/F)

5. Use the _____ tool to reference a larger section off a building section.

## Review Questions:
The following questions may be assigned by your instructor as a way to assess your knowledge of this section. Your instructor has the answers to the review questions.

1. The visibility of the crop window can be controlled. (T/F)

2. It's not possible to draw a leader (line w/ arrow) with out placing text. (T/F)

3. When a section mark is added to a view, all the other related views automatically get a section mark added to it. (T/F)

4. It is possible to modify objects (like doors, windows & ceilings) in section views. (T/F)

5. You cannot adjust the "depth of view" (width) using the crop window. (T/F)

6. What is the first thing you should do after placing a section tag?

   _____

7. If the text appears to be excessively large in a section view, the views

   _____ _____ is probably set incorrectly.

8. The abbreviation M.O. stands for _____ _____.

9. Describe what happens when you double-click on the section bubble:

   _____ .

10. Revit provides _____ different leader options within the text command.

*Self-Exam Answers:*
**1** – T, **2** – T, **3** – F, **4** – T, **5** - callout

**Notes:**

# Lesson 9
# Office Building: FLOOR PLAN FEATURES::

This lesson explores the various "features," if you will, of a floor plan, such as toilet room layouts (i.e., fixtures & partitions), and cabinets and casework (e.g., reception counters & custom cabinets). Additionally, you will look at placing pre-drawn furniture into your project.

## Exercise 9-1:
## Toilet room layouts

Toilet room layouts involve placing water closets (toilets), toilet partitions and sinks. These rooms have many code issues related primarily to handicapped accessibility. These codes vary from state to state (and even city to city).

You will start this exercise by loading several components to be placed into your project.

1.  Open ex8-4.rvt and **Save As ex9-1.rvt**.

2.  Select the **Component** tool and load the following items into the current project:
    **Local Files** *(i.e., on your hard drive)*
    a. Plumbing Fixtures\**Toilet-Comercial-Wall-3D.rfa**
    b. Plumbing Fixtures\**Urinal-Wall-3D**
    **Online Files** *(i.e., Revit's Web Library on internet)*
    c. Plumbing Fixtures\**Sink-Wall-Rectangular**
    d. Specialty Equipment\Toilet Room Specialties\**Grab Bar-3D**
    e. " "\**Toilet Stall-Accessible-Front-Braced-3D**
    f. " "\**Toilet Stall-Braced-3D**
    g. " "\**Urinal Screen-3D**
    h. " "\**Grab Bar-3D**

These files represent various predefined families that will be used to design the toilet room. It is possible to create custom families for non-typical conditions.

**Figure 9-1** shows an example of the various families available for Toilet Stalls on Revit's web site.

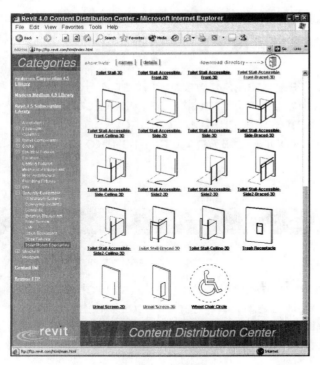

**Figure 9-1** Toilet stalls online

3. Switch to **Level 1** view.

The next step will be to place the toilet stalls.

4. With the Component tool selected, pick **Toilet Stall-Accessible-Front-Braced-3D: 60" x 60" Clear** from the type selector.

5. Zoom in to the toilet rooms (north of the elevator).

6. **Place** the toilet stall as shown and then move into place using the **Move** tool and your snaps. (Figure 9-2)

Once you move the toilet stall north, you will have your first stall in place.

Next, you will place two standard size toilet stalls.

7. Place two toilet stalls (**Toilet Stall-Braced-3D: 36" x 60" Clear**) as shown in Figure 9-3.

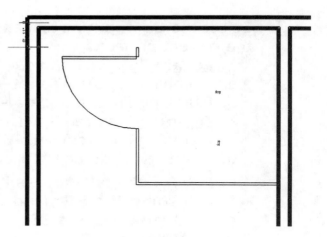

**Figure 9-2** Accessible Toilet stall

As with most projects, you will need to modify the model as you develop the design. In this case we notice that toilets that are back-to-back and stacked on each floor will require a thicker wall to accommodate the fixture brackets (W.C.'s are not hung on the wall by light gage metal studs) and larger piping. You will make this adjustment next.

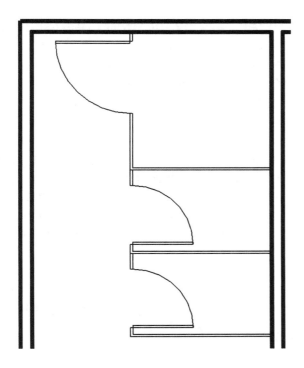

**Figure 9-3** Toilet stalls placed

8. Select the middle wall and the west wall and **Move** them **6"** to the west.

9. **Move** the far east wall (of the two toilet rooms) **6"** to the east.

10. Add an additional **4 7/8"** gyp. bd. wall as shown in **Figure 9-4**.

11. Modify the north wall of the elevator shaft to have furring & gyp. bd. on the toilet room side. *Tip: use the wall type you created for the stair shafts.*

12. Add the additional components as shown in **Figure 9-4**.

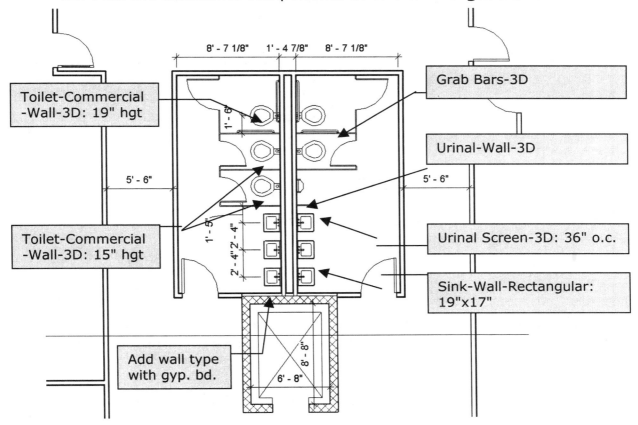

**Figure 9-4** Toilet room layout

As mentioned previously, building codes vary by location. The toilets in the accessible stall area are typically mounted higher than the typical fixtures. When a room has more than one urinal, one is usually required to be mounted lower for accessibility. Another example is that Minnesota requires a separate vertical grab bar above the horizontal grab bar on the wall next to the toilet.

You will now copy the revised walls and toilet room layout to the other levels. The elevator shaft extends through each floor, so you will not have to copy that wall. Looking at the upper levels you can see the revised elevator shaft wall and the old wall layout (Figure 9-5). It will be easier to delete the stud walls rather than modify the existing walls.

13. Delete the walls, per **Figure 9-6**, for levels 2 and 3.

14. **Copy** the walls and toilet room layout to the clipboard and **Paste Aligned** to levels 2 and 3.

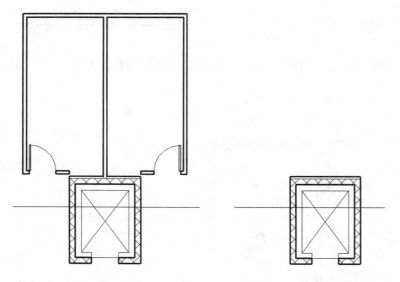

**Figure 9-5** Walls on upper levels          **Figure 9-6** Walls deleted

## Interior Elevation view:

Next, you will set up an interior elevation view for the Men's Toilet Room. You will also add a mirror above the sinks in elevation view.

15. Switch to **Level 1** and Place an **Elevation** bubble looking towards the wet wall (wall with fixtures on it). (Figure 9-10)

16. Rename the new view to: **Men's Toilet – Typical** in the *Project Browser*.

17. Switch to the new view. Adjust the Crop Region so the concrete slab is not visible. Your view should look like Figure 9-11.

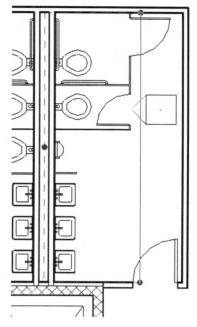

You should see the building section reference as shown in Figure 9-11. This would not typically be shown in an interior elevation view, especially because it does not intersect the elevation view. You will remove the reference in the next step. You cannot simply delete it, because that will remove it from all views and delete the section.

**Figure 9-10** Elevation tag added

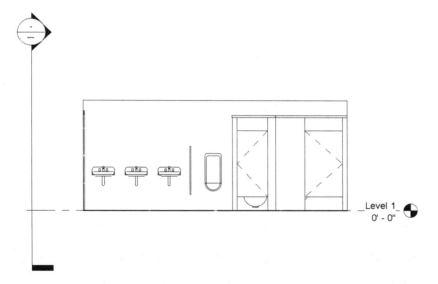

**Figure 9-11** Men's Toilet – Typical view

18. Click on the section reference to select it, and then right-click and pick **Hide Annotation in View** from the pop-up menu. (Figure 9-12)

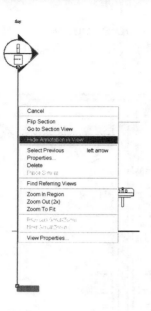

19. Load component *Specialty Equipment\Toilet Room Specialties\***Mirror.rfa** from the Online Revit library.

20. While in the interior elevation view, place a **72" x 48" Mirror** on the wall above the sinks. Use the *Align* tool to align the mirror with the middle sink. (Figure 9-13)

21. Add the notes and dimensions shown in Figure 9-13. Adjust the heights and locations of the fixtures / components as required.

**Figure 9-12** Hide annotation

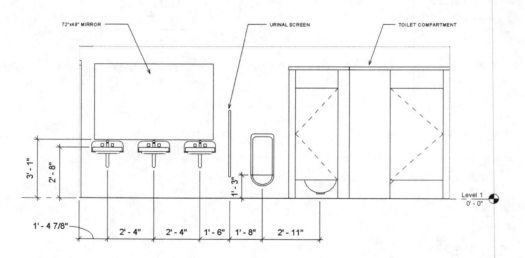

**Figure 9-13** Updated interior elevation

**FYI:** keep in mind that many of the symbols that come with Revit (or any program for that matter) are not necessarily drawn or reviewed by an architect. The point is that the default values, such as mounting heights, may not meet ADA, national, state or local codes. Items like the mirror have a maximum height off the floor to the reflective surface that Revit's standard components may not comply with. However, as you apply local codes to these families, you can reuse them in the future.

## Adjusting the Reflected Ceiling Plan:

Because you added a wall in the east toilet room, the definition of the room that the reflected ceiling plan uses is incorrect. You will adjust that next. You will have similar problems on levels 2 and 3 because you deleted walls and then pasted new walls.

22. Switch to **Level 1 RCP**. (Figure 9-14)

23. Hide the Elevation tag from this view.

24. Delete the ceiling in the Men's Toilet room.

25. Place a new ceiling to fit within the room.

26. Select the ceiling grid in the atrium, and then pick **Edit Sketch** to adjust the reference lines for the perimeter of the ceiling grid in the atrium area. *FYI: you could have used this method for steps 24/25 as well.* (Figure 9-15)

27. Correct the ceiling on level 2 and 3.

28. **Save** your project as **ex9-1.rvt**.

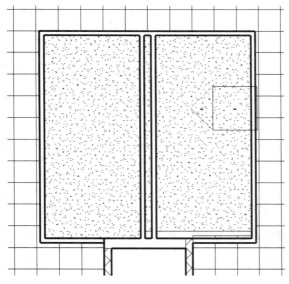

**Figure 9-14** Level 1 RCP

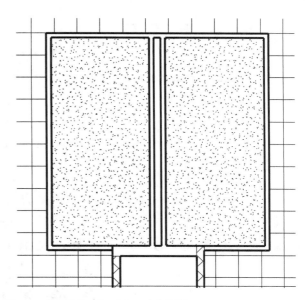

**Figure 9-15** Revised Level 1 RCP

## Exercise 9-2:
## Cabinets

In this exercise you will look at adding cabinets and casework to your project. As usual, Revit provides several pre-defined families to be placed into the project.

### Placing cabinets:

You will add base and wall cabinets in a break room on level 1.

1. Open ex9-1.rvt and **Save As ex9-2.rvt**.

2. Switch to **level 1** view and zoom into the area shown in **Figure 9-16**.

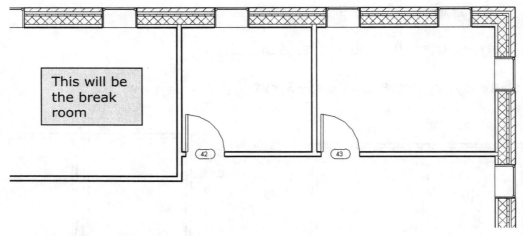

**Figure 9-16** Level 1 – north-east corner

1. Load the following components into the project (*all local files*):
   a. \Casework\Domestic Kitchen\**Countertop w Sink Hole**
   b. \ " "\**Base Cabinet-Double Door Sink Unit**
   c. \ " "\**Base Cabinet-Single Door**
   d. \ " "\**Base Cabinet-4 Drawers**
   e. \ " "\**Upper Cabinet-Double Door**
   f. \Pluming Fixtures\**Sink Kitchen-Single**
   g. Specialty Equipment\Domestic\**Refrigerator**

You are now ready to place the cabinets into your floor plan.

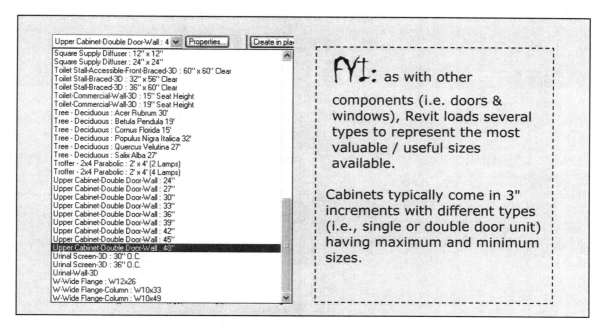

2. With the Component tool selected, pick **Base Cabinet-4 Drawers: 24"** from the *Type Selector* on the *Options Bar*.

3. Place the cabinet as shown in **Figure 9-17**. *TIP: the control arrows are on the front side of the cabinet; you may need the rotate the cabinet.*

4. Place the other two base cabinets as shown in **Figure 9-18**, with a 24" single door cabinet in the middle and a 48" sink base to the north end.

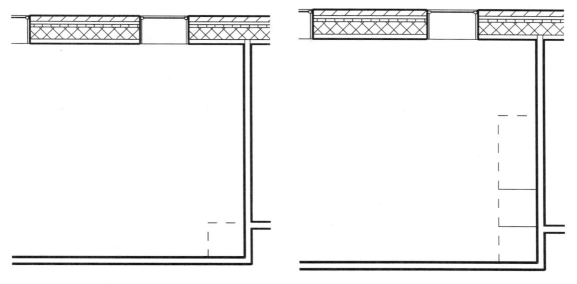

**Figure 9-17** First cabinet placed

**Figure 9-18** Three base cabinets placed

5.  Add the remaining items as shown in Figure 9-19; be sure to use snaps *(e.g., place sink to one side, use move and snap to a mid-point of the sink bowl, and then to the mid-point of the same line representing the hole in the countertop)*.

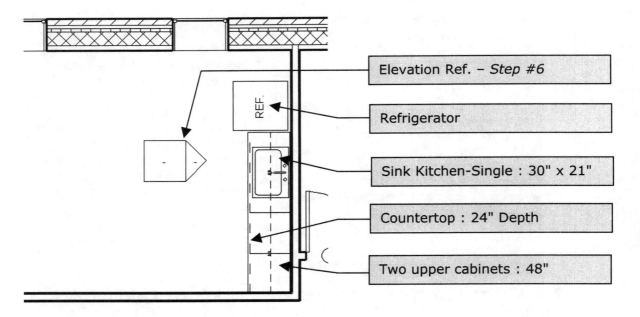

**Figure 9-19** Completed plan view

6.  Add an elevation tag to setup the interior elevation view. (Figure 9-19)

7.  Rename the new elevation view to **Break Room (east)**.

8.  Switch to the new view, **Break Room (east)**.

9.  Adjust the **Crop Region** so the slab on grade is not visible.

10. Your drawing should look like **Figure 9-20**.

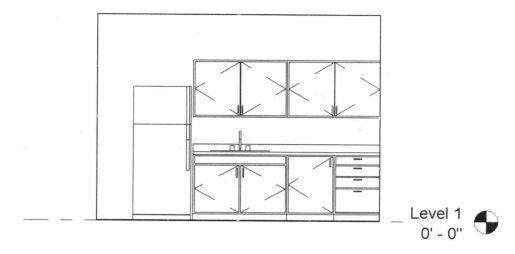

Level 1
0' - 0"

**Figure 9-20** Interior elevation

You will add notes and dimensions to the elevation. You can also add 2D line work to the elevation.

11. Set the view scale to **½" = 1'-0"**.

12. Add the notes and dimensions per **Figure 9-21**.

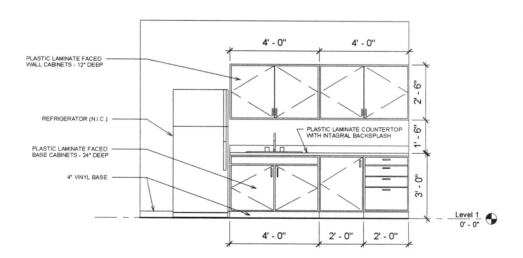

**Figure 9-21** Interior elevation with annotations

13. Use the **Lines** tool to draw the line behind the refrigerator, indicating the vinyl base.

When you select the **Lines** tool, Revit will ask you what plane you want to draw on (Figure 9-22). This will allow Revit to restrict all your line work to a particular plane. Otherwise you would not know exactly at what depth the lines would be drawn on.

14. Select **Pick a Plane** (Figure 9-22) and then pick the wall in the elevation view (use the TAB key and make sure the tool tip lists the wall before picking the plane. *TIP: If you are prompted to switch to a different view, you selected the wrong plane. Click cancel and try again.*

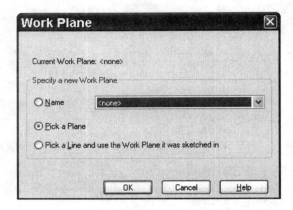

**Figure 9-22** Work Plane prompt

15. Draw the line, snap to the endpoint of the base cabinet toe kick.

16. Select the line and in Properties, change the *Line Style* to **Thin Lines**.

17. **Save** your project as **ex9-2.rvt**.

## Exercise 9-3:
## Furniture

This lesson will cover the steps required to lay out office furniture. The processes are identical to those previously covered for toilets and cabinets.

Loading the necessary families:

1.  Open ex9-2.rvt and **Save As ex9-3.rvt**.

2.  Select the Component tool and load the following items into the current project:
    **Local Files** *(i.e., on your hard drive)*
    a.  Furniture System\\**Work Station Cubicle.rfa**
    b.  Furniture System\\**Work Station Desktops**
    c.  Furniture\\**Sofa-Pensi**
    d.  Furniture\\**Chair-Breuer**
    e.  Furniture\\**Chair-Executive**
    f.  Furniture\\**Chair-Task Arms**
    g.  Furniture\\**Table-Round**
    **Online Files** *(i.e., Revit's Web Library on internet)*
    h.  Specialty Equipment\\Office Equipment\\**Copier-Floor**

These files represent various predefined families that will be used to design the offices.

---

*TIP:* you can set the View mode for the Open dialog box (which is displayed when you click *Load from Library*. One option is Thumbnail mode; this displays a small thumbnail image for each file in the current folder. This makes it easier to see the many symbols and drawings that are available for insertion.

**Above:** View set to List mode

**Right:** View set to Thumbnail mode

---

## Designing the office furniture layout:

3.  Switch to the **Level 3** view.

4.  Place the furniture as shown in Figure 9-23.
    *TIP: use snaps to assure accuracy; use rotate and mirror as required.*

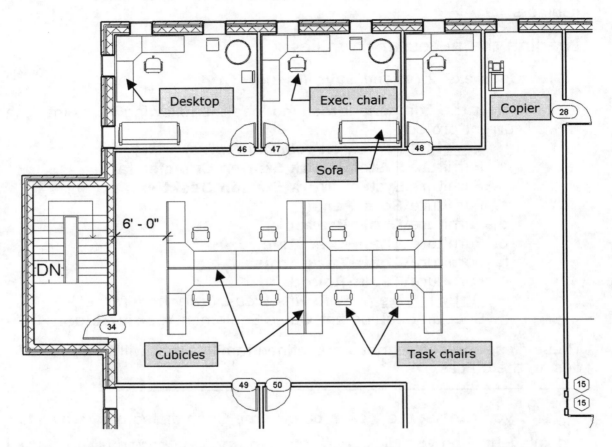

**Figure 9-23** Level 3 – furniture layout

The cubicles in the open office area should be centered in the north-south direction. The cubicle partitions should overlap so only one partition is visible. The items not labeled in Figure 9-23 should be compared to the families listed in step 2; it will be obvious as to what the items are.

## 3D view of office layout:

Next you will look at a 3D view of your office area. This involves adjusting the visibility of the roof and skylights.

5.  Switch to the **Default 3D** view.

6.  Right click anywhere in the drawing window and select **View Properties** from the pop-up list.

7.  Click **Edit** next to the *Visibility* parameter.

8.  Uncheck the Roof category and click OK twice.

The roof should not be visible now. However, you should still see the skylights floating in space. You will make those disappear next.

9.  Click the Hide/Isolate tool from the View toolbar.

You should see the dialog box in **Figure 9-24** show up in the lower left corner of your screen. This allows you to isolate an object (so it's the only thing on the screen) or hide it (so the object is temporarily not visible).

To hide or isolate something, first select the object(s), and then click either the *Hide Selected* or the *Isolate Selected* button. Once something is hidden or isolated, the *Reset* button becomes active. Clicking the *Reset* button restores the view to its original state.

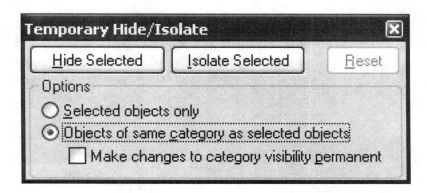

**Figure 9-24** Hide/Isolate dialog

10. Click **Objects of same category as selected objects** in the dialog. (Figure 9-24)

11. Select one of the skylights in the 3D view.

12. Click the **Hide Selected** button.

13. Adjust your 3D view to look similar to **Figure 9-25**.

You will now restore the original visibility settings for the 3D view.

14. Click the **Restore** button on the Temporary Hide/Isolate dialog.
    *TIP: if the dialog box is not visible, click the icon again.*

15. Reset the 3D view's visibility settings so the roof is visible.

16. **Save** your project as **ex9-3.rvt**.

Notice the furniture and toilet rooms are represented in 3D.

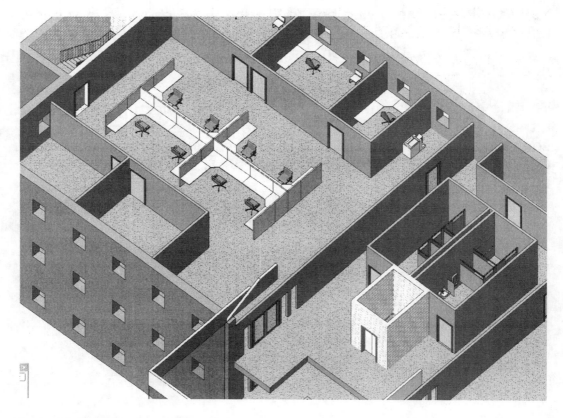

**Figure 9-25** 3D view w/ roof not visible

## Exercise 9-4:
## Adding Guardrails

This lesson will cover the steps required to layout guardrails. The processes are identical to those previously cover for toilets and cabinets.

### Adding a guardrail to the Atrium:

1. Open ex9-3.rvt and **Save As ex9-4.rvt**.

2. Switch to Level 2 view.

3. From the *Modeling* tab select **Railing**.

4. **Zoom** into the Atrium area (south of the elevator).

At this point you will draw a line representing the path of the guardrail. The railing is offset to one side of the line, similar to Walls. However, you do not have the Loc Line option as you do with the Wall tool, so you have to draw the railing in a certain direction to get the railing to be on the floor and not hovering in space just beyond the floor edge.

5. Draw a line along the edge of the floor as shown in **Figure 9-26** *TIP: Select Chain from the Options Bar to draw the railing with fewer picks.*

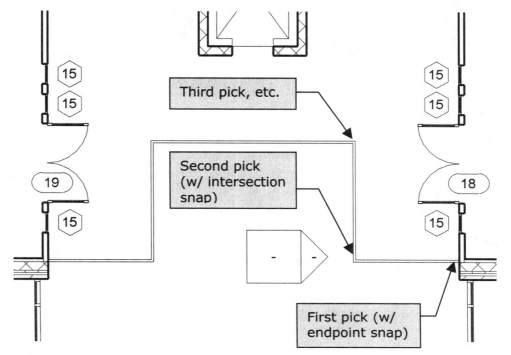

**Figure 9-26** Adding guardrail – Level 2

6. Click **Finish Sketch** from the *Design Bar*.

The railing has now been drawn. In the next step you will switch to a 3D view and see how to quickly change the railing style. This will also involve changing the height of the railing. Most building codes require the railing height be 42" when the drop to the adjacent surface is more than 30"; this is called a guardrail.

7. Switch to the **Default 3D** view.

8. Zoom into the railing shown on Level 2, looking at it through the curtainwall. (Notice the railing style – Figure 9-27.)

**Figure 9-27** Added railing – 3D view

9. Select the railing. You may have to use the Tab key to cycle through the various selection options.

10. With the railing selected, select the various railing types available in the Type Selector on the options bar. When finished make sure **Railing: Guardrail – Pipe** is selected. (Figure 9-28)

**Figure 9-28** Options for selected railing

Your railing should now look like Figure 9-29. Notice that a handrail was added to the railing. You should also notice that the handrail is on the wrong side of the guardrail. You will adjust that next.

**Figure 9-29** Railing with new style

11. Switch to the **Level 2** plan view and select the railing.

12. Click on the **Control Arrows** to flip the railing orientation.

13. You can switch back to the 3D view to see the change.

14. Finally, from the Level 2 plan view, **Copy** the railing to the clipboard and **Paste** it into the Level 3 view.

15. **Save** your project as **ex9-4.rvt**.

## Self-Exam:

The following questions can be used as a way to check your knowledge of this lesson. The answers can be found on the last page of this section.

1. The toilet room fixtures are preloaded in the template file. (T/F)

2. You do not need to be connected to the internet when you click on the *Load from Web* button in the Load from Library dialog box. (T/F)

3. The Revit items are not always in compliance with codes. (T/F)

4. You can draw 2D lines on the wall in an interior elevation view. (T/F)

5. Use the _____ tool to copy fixtures to other floors

## Review Questions:

The following questions may be assigned by your instructor as a way to assess your knowledge of this section. Your instructor has the answers to the review questions.

1. Revit provides several different styles of toilet stalls for placement. (T/F)

2. Most of the time Revit automatically updates the ceiling when walls are moved, but occasionally you have to manually make revisions. (T/F)

3. It is not possible to draw dimensions on an interior elevation view. (T/F)

4. Cabinets typically come in 6" increments. (T/F)

5. Base cabinets automatically have a countertop on them. (T/F)

6. What can you adjust so the concrete slab does not show in section?

   _____

7. How does Revit determine where to place 2D line in an elevation view (based on the example in this lesson)?

   _____

8. What is the current size of your Revit Project?

   _____

9. What should you use to assure accuracy when placing furniture?

   _____

10. You use the _____ tool to make various components temporarily invisible.

# Lesson 10
# Office Building: ESTIMATE and SCHEDULES::

You will continue to learn the powerful features available in Revit. This includes cost estimates to make sure your project is on budget. The ability to create parametric schedules is also very useful, you can delete a door number on a schedule and Revit will delete the corresponding door from the plan.

## Exercise 10-1:
## Cost Estimate using RS Means CostWorks module

You will review the estimating feature available in Revit. This is done using the RS Means CostWorks software built into Revit. RS Means is the industry standard resource for estimating in an architectural office.

Currently, the architect prepares an estimate using the RS Means books (or stand alone CostWorks software) and recent, similar projects. Revit is not at the point to replace a full estimate, but likely will be in the near future.

### Generate a Preliminary Cost Report:

Note: the CostWorks plug-in is installed automatically. However, there is an option to not install it during the initial installation. It needs to be installed to complete this exercise.

1.  Open ex9-4.rvt and **Save As ex10-1.rvt**.

2.  From the **View** pull-down menu, select **New → Cost Report**.

3.  Click on the **Building Type** button. *Notice the other buttons are grayed-out because you need to set the options under Building Type before you can proceed to the next button.* (Figure10-1)

You are now looking at the *Preliminary Cost Report* view. You can think of this view the same way you think about other views, like interior elevations or floor plans. Instead of a graphical view, you see a numeric view based on the building model. You should be able to see this new view under *Report* in the *Project Browser*.

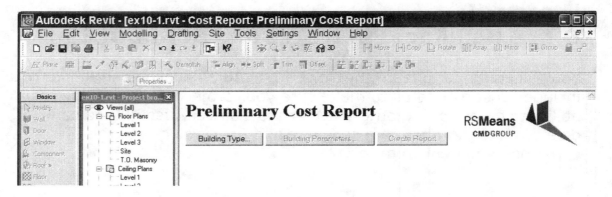

**Figure 10-1** Cost report view

4. Adjust the setting for the Building Type as follows: (Figure 10-2)
   a. Building category: **Commercial**
   b. Building type: **Office: 2-4 Story**
   c. Exterior wall type: **Face Brick with Concrete Block Backup**
   d. Structural system: **Steel Joists**
   e. Location code: **See the next step, below**

Leave the other setting at the defaults.

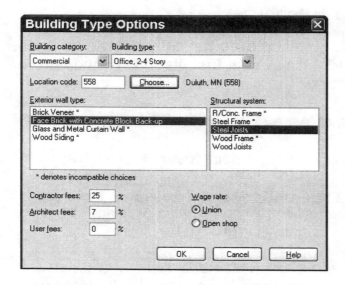

**Figure 10-2** Building Type Options dialog

**FYI:**

**Wage rate** indicates if the contractor is Union or not.

**User fees** provides a place to enter a fee the owner may charge itself for each building project. For example, a university's building construction administration department typically charges a fee, for each project, to cover its costs of operation.

5. Click the **Choose...** button for the *Location code*.

6. Select your state and city and then click **OK**. (Figure 10-3)

**Figure 10-3** Building Location selector

7. Click **OK** to close the *Building Type Options* dialog.

8. Next, click the **Building Parameters** button in the *Preliminary Cost Report* view.

9. **Uncheck** the **T.O. Masonry** level in the Non-basement story levels area. (Figure 10-4)

10. Click **OK**.

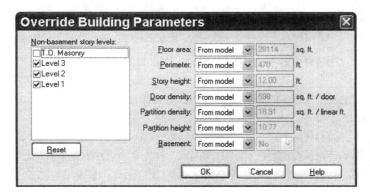

**Figure 10-4** Override Building Parameters

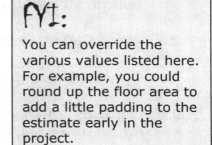

FYI:

You can override the various values listed here. For example, you could round up the floor area to add a little padding to the estimate early in the project.

11. Click **Create Report**

Revit now displays the Cost Report generated by *CostWorks*. You can scroll to the bottom to see the project is estimated to cost a little over $3 million dollars (may vary with location factor). (Figure 10-5)

| | Sub-Total | 80.60 | 2,265,975.00 | 100% |
|---|---|---|---|---|
| GENERAL CONDITIONS (Overhead & Profit) | **25.00%** | 20.15 | 566,500.00 | |
| ARCHITECTURAL FEES | **7.00%** | 7.06 | 198,500.00 | |
| USER FEES | **0.00%** | 0.00 | 0.00 | |
| TOTAL BUILDING COST | | 107.81 | 3,030,975.00 | |

**Figure 10-5** Preliminary Cost Report view totals (partial view)

The Preliminary Cost Report view is now listed in the Project Browser under Reports. You can open this view at any time and click the Update Report button to update the estimate as the project progresses.

Revit provides an export option that allows you to export the cost estimate to an HTML file. With this file you could place it on the internet for a client to see. You can also bring the HTML data into Excel for future manipulation of the estimate data.

## Export the Preliminary Cost Report to MS Excel:

12. With the *Preliminary Cost Report* view set current, Select **File → Export → Cost Report**.

13. **Save** the file with a name and location you will remember.

14. Open **MS Internet Explorer** and click **Open** from the **File** pull-down menu and then click **Browse**.

15. Press **Ctrl-A** to select all the data in the HTML file.

16. Open **MS Excel** and select **Paste** from the **Edit** menu.

You can now make changes to the more detailed estimate, including the many assumptions CostWorks made regarding your project in MS Excel. You would have to set the formulas up so the columns would add up. (Figure 10-6)

17. **Save** your Revit project as **ex10-1.rvt**

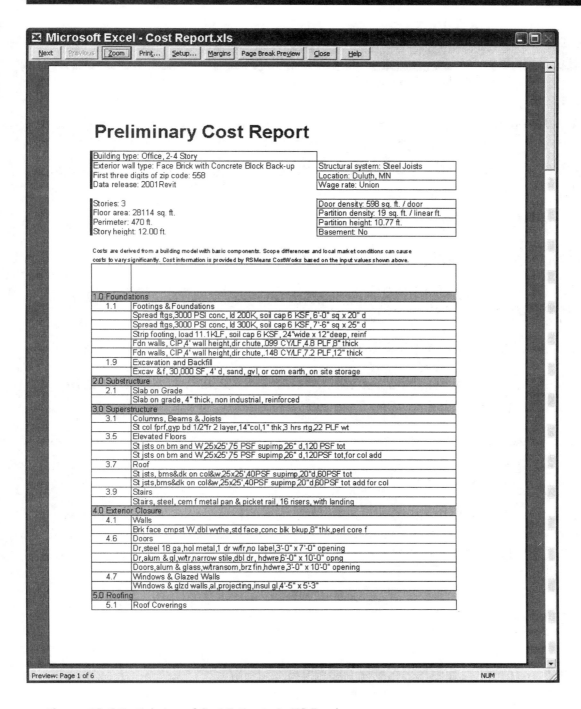

**Figure 10-6** Partial view of Cost Estimate in MS Excel

## Exercise 10-2:
## Room and Door Tags

This exercise will look at adding room tags and door tags to your plans. As you insert doors, Revit adds tags to them automatically. However, if you copy or mirror a door you can lose the tag and have to add it.

### Adding Room Tags:

You will add a Room Tag to each room on your Level 1 floor plan.

⊖ Room Tag

1. From the *Drafting Tab* on the *Design Bar*, select **Room Tag**.

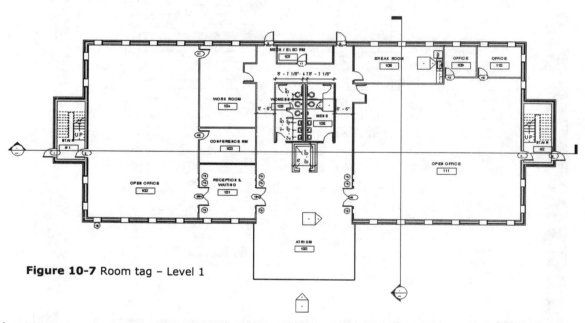

**Figure 10-7** Room tag – Level 1

Placing a room tag is similar to placing a ceiling in the reflected ceiling plan; as you move your cursor over a room, the room (perimeter) highlights. When the room you want to place a room nametag in is highlighted, you click to place the tag in that room.

2. Place your cursor within the atrium area and place a room tag. (Figure 10-7)

By default, Revit will simply label the space 'Room' and number it '1.' You will change these to something different.

3.  Press **Esc** or select **Modify** to cancel the Room Tag command.

4.  Click on the *Room Tag* you just placed to select it.

5.  Now click on the room name label to change it; enter **Atrium**.

6.  Now click on the room number to change it; enter **100**.

7.  Enter Room Tags for each room on Level 1, incrementing each room number by 1. (Figure 10-7)

The stair shafts typically are numbered Stair #1, Stair #2, etc. The same number is then placed on each level. This is because stair shafts are really one tall room and the finishes would apply to the entire shaft, not each floor.

8.  Add Room Tags to levels 2 and 3. The numbering for level 2 should start with 200 and level 3 should start with 300.

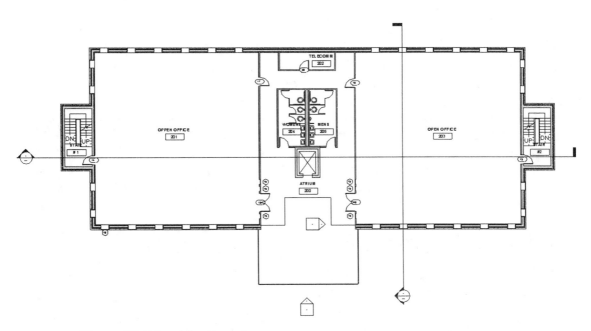

**Figure 10-8** Level 2 – Room tags

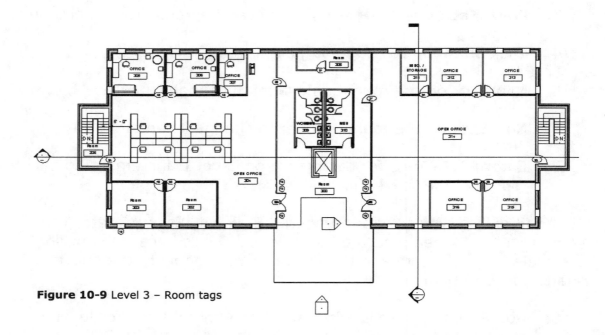

**Figure 10-9** Level 3 – Room tags

## Adding Door Tags:

Next you will add Door Tags to any doors that are missing them. Additionally, you will adjust the door numbers to correspond to the room numbers.

Revit numbers the doors in the order they are placed into the drawing. This would make it difficult to locate a door by its door number if door number 1 was on level 1 and door number 2 was on level 3, etc. Typically, a door number is the same as the room the door swings into. For example, if a door swung into an office numbered 304, the door number would also be 304. If the office had two doors into it, the doors would be numbered 304A and 304B.

9. Switch to **Level 1** view.

10. Click the **Tag** button on the *Drafting* tab. (Figure 10-10)

Notice as you move your cursor around the screen Revit displays a tag, for items that can have tags, when the cursor is over it. When you click the mouse is when Revit actually places a tag.

**Figure 10-10**
Drafting tab

11. **Uncheck** the **Leader** option on the *Options Bar*.

12. Place a door tag for each door that does not have a tag, do this for each level.

13. Renumber all the door tags to correspond to the room they open into; do this for each level. (Figure 10-11)
*Remember to click Modify, select the Tag and then click on the number to edit it.*

> *TIP:*
>
> ***Tag All Not Tagged...*** this tool allows you to quickly tag all the objects of a selected type (e.g. doors) at one time.
>
> After selecting the tool, you select the type of object from a list and specify whether or not you want a leader. When you click OK, Revit tags all the untagged doors in that view.

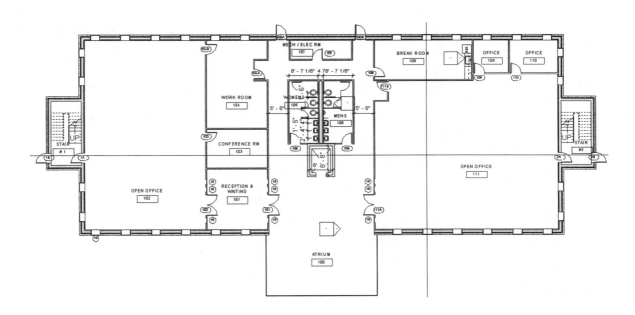

**Figure 10-11** Level 1 – door tags

14. **Save** your project as **ex10-2.rvt**.

## Exercise 10-3:
## Generate a Door Schedule

This exercise will look at creating a door schedule based on the information currently available in the building model (i.e., the tags).

### Create a Door Schedule view:

A door schedule is simply another view of the building model. However, this view displays numerical data rather than graphical data. Just like a graphical view, if you change the view it changes all the other related views. For example, if you delete a door number from the schedule, the door is deleted from the plans and elevations.

1. Open ex10-2.rvt and **Save As ex10-3.rvt**.

2. Select the **Schedule/Quantities** button from the *View* tab on the *Design Bar*.

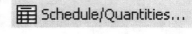

3. Select **Doors** under *Category* and then click **OK**. (Figure 10-12)

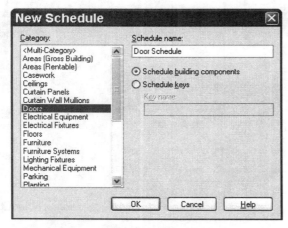

**Figure 10-12** New Schedule dialog

You should now be in the Schedule Properties dialog where you specify what information is displayed in the schedule, how it is sorted and the text format.

4. On the **Fields** tab, add the information you want displayed in the schedule. Select the following: (Figure 10-13)
   a. Mark
   b. Width
   c. Height
   d. Frame Material
   e. Frame Height
   f. Fire Rating

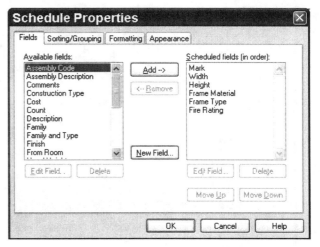

As noted in the dialog, the fields added to the list on the right are in the order they will be in the schedule view. Use the *Move Up* and *Move Down* buttons to adjust the order.

**Figure 10-13** Schedule Properties - Fields

5. On the **Sorting/Grouping** tab, set the schedule to be sorted by the Mark (i.e., door number) in ascending order. (Figure 10-14)

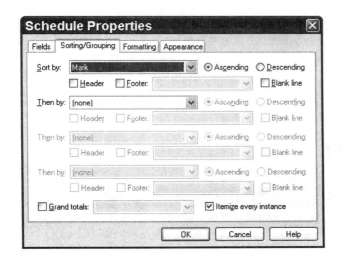

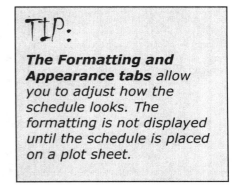

*TIP:*

**The Formatting and Appearance tabs** *allow you to adjust how the schedule looks. The formatting is not displayed until the schedule is placed on a plot sheet.*

**Figure 10-14** Schedule Properties - Sorting

6. Click the **OK** button to generate the schedule view.

You should now have a schedule similar to Figure 10-15.

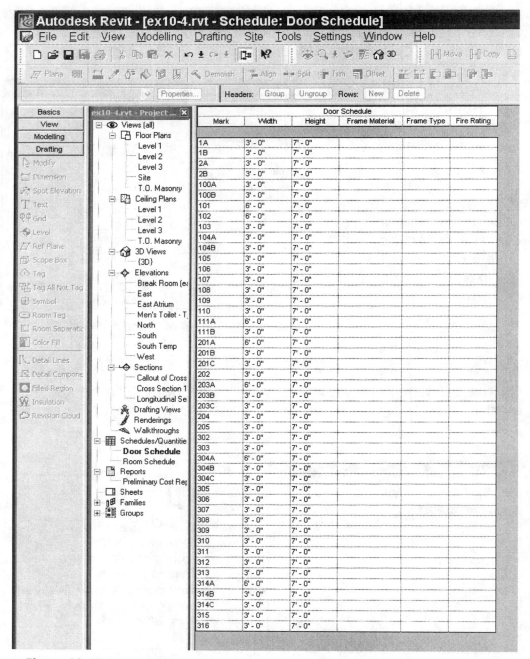

**Figure 10-15** Door schedule view

Next you will see how adding a door to the plan automatically updates the door schedule. Likewise, deleting a door number from the schedule deletes the door from the plan.

7.    Switch to the **Level 1** view.

8.  Add a door as shown in **Figure 10-16**; number the door **111C**.

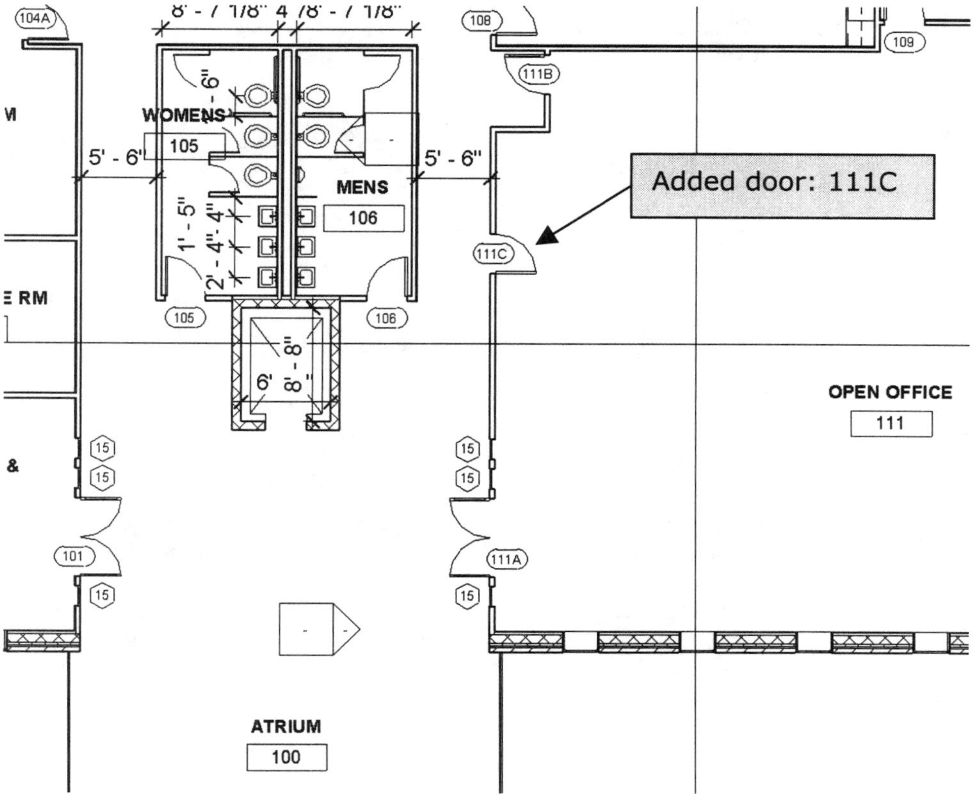

**Figure 10-16** Level 1 – door added

9.  Switch to the **Door Schedule** view, under Schedules/Quantities in the *Project Browser*. Notice door 111C was added. (Figure 10-17)

| | | |
|---|---|---|
| 109 | 3' - 0" | 7' - 0" |
| 110 | 3' - 0" | 7' - 0" |
| 111A | 6' - 0" | 7' - 0" |
| 111B | 3' - 0" | 7' - 0" |
| 111C | 3' - 0" | 7' - 0" |
| 201A | 6' - 0" | 7' - 0" |
| 201B | 3' - 0" | 7' - 0" |

**Figure 10-17** Updated door schedule

Next you will delete door 111C from the door schedule view.

10. Click in the cell with the number 111C.

11. Now click the **Delete** button from the Options Bar. (Figure 10-18)

**Figure 10-18** Options Bar for the door schedule view

You will get an alert. Revit is telling you that the actual door will be deleted from the project model. (Figure 10-19)

12. Click **OK** to delete the door. (Figure 10-19)

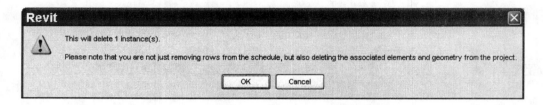

**Figure 10-19** Revit alert message

13. Switch back to the **Level 1** view and notice that door 111C has been deleted from the project model.

14. **Save** your project as **ex10-3.rvt**.

## Exercise 10-4:
## Generate a Room Finish Schedule

In this exercise you will create a Room Finish schedule. The process is similar to the previous exercise. You will also create a color-coded plan based on information associated with the room tag.

### Create a Room Finish Schedule:

1.  Open ex10-3.rvt and **Save As ex10-4.rvt**.

2.  Select the **Schedule/Quantities** button from the *View* tab on the *Design Bar*.

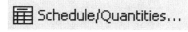

3.  Select **Room** under *Category* and then click **OK**. (Figure 10-20)

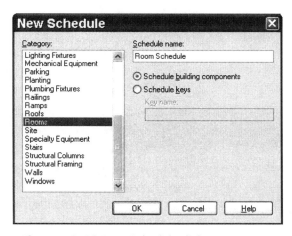

**Figure 10-20** New Schedule dialog

4.  In the **Fields** tab of the *Schedule Properties* dialog, add the following fields to be scheduled (Figure 10-21):
    a.  Number
    b.  Name
    c.  Base Finish
    d.  Floor Finish
    e.  Wall Finish
    f.  Ceiling Finish
    g.  Area

Area is not typically listed on a room finish schedule. However, you will add it to your schedule to see the various options Revit allows.

5.  On the **Sorting/Grouping** tab set the schedule to be sorted by the **Number** field.

6.  On the **Appearance** tab, select **Bold** for the header font. (Figure 10-21)

7.  Select **OK** to generate the **Room Schedule**.

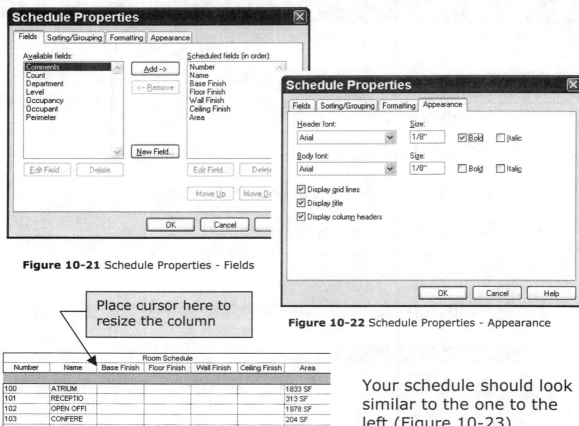

**Figure 10-21** Schedule Properties - Fields

**Figure 10-22** Schedule Properties - Appearance

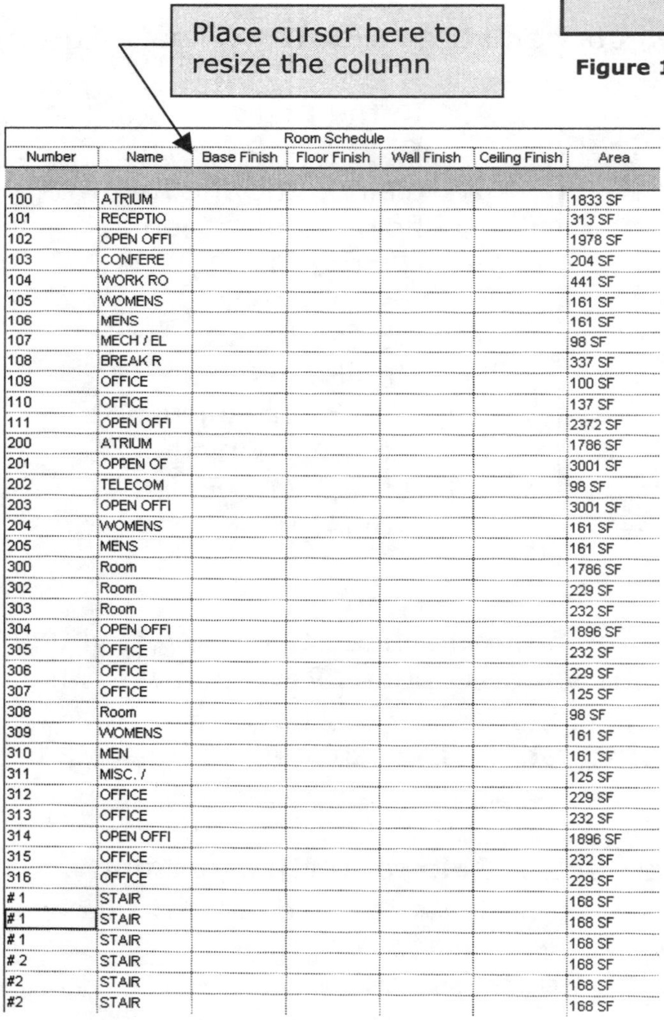

Place cursor here to resize the column

**Figure 10-23** Room Schedule view

Your schedule should look similar to the one to the left (Figure 10-23).

8.  Resize the Name column so all the room names are visible. Place the cursor between the Name and Base Finish and drag to the right until all the names are visible. (Figure 10-23)

The formatting (i.e., Bold header text) will not show up until the schedule is placed on a plot sheet.

## Modifying & Populating a Room Schedule:

Like the door schedule, the room schedule is a tabular view of the building model. So you can change the room name on the schedule or in the plans.

9.  In the **Room Schedule** view, change the name for room 308 (this should be the room directly north of the toilet rooms) to **MECH / ELEC RM**. *TIP: Click on the current room name and then click on the down-arrow that appears. This gives you a list of all the existing names in the current schedule.*

10. Switch to the **Level 3** view to see the updated room tag.

You can quickly enter finish information to several rooms at one time. You will do this next.

11. In the Level 3 plan view, select the Room Tags for all private offices (9 total). (Figure 10-24) *REMEMBER: hold the Ctrl key down to select multiple objects.*

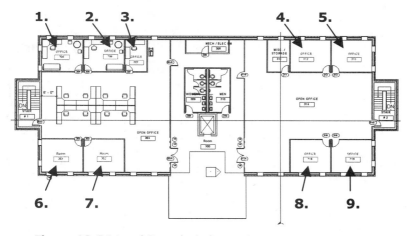

**Figure 10-24** Level 3 – selected room tags

12. Click the **Properties** button on the *Options Bar*.

The Parameters listed here are the same as the Fields available for display in the room schedule. When more than one tag is displayed and a parameter is not the same (e.g., different names), that value field is left blank. Otherwise, the values are displayed for the selected tag. Next you will enter values for the finishes.

13. If the *Name* field is blank enter **OFFICE**, so the nine rooms are labeled office.

14. Enter the following for the finishes (Figure 10-25):
    a. Base Finish:       **Wood**
    b. Ceiling Finish:    **ACT 1**     *(ACT = acoustic ceiling tile)*
    c. Wall Finish:       **VWC 1**     *(VWC = vinyl wall covering)*
    d. Floor Finish:      **Carpet 1**

15. Click **OK**.

16. Switch back to the **Room Schedule** view to see the automatic updates. (Figure 10-26)

You can also enter data directly into the Room Schedule view.

17. Enter the following data for the Men's and Women's toilet rooms:
    a. Base:      COVED CT
    b. Ceiling:   Gyp. Bd.
    c. Wall:      CT
    d. Floor:     CT

Hopefully, in the near future, Revit will be able to enter the finishes based on the wall, floor and ceiling type previously created!

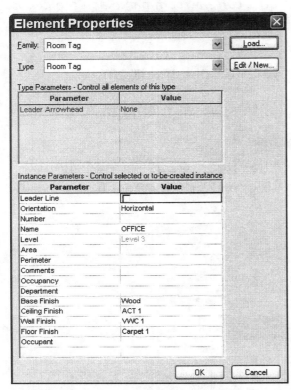

**Figure 10-25** Element Properties – Room Tags

**TIP:**

**You can add fields and adjust formatting** *anytime by right-clicking on the schedule view and selecting View Properties. This gives you the same options that were available when you created the schedule.*

| | | | | | | |
|---|---|---|---|---|---|---|
| 204 | WOMENS | | | | | 161 SF |
| 205 | MENS | | | | | 161 SF |
| 300 | Room | | | | | 1786 SF |
| 302 | OFFICE | Wood | Carpet 1 | VWC 1 | ACT 1 | 229 SF |
| 303 | OFFICE | Wood | Carpet 1 | VWC 1 | ACT 1 | 232 SF |
| 304 | OPEN OFFICE | | | | | 1896 SF |
| 305 | OFFICE | Wood | Carpet 1 | VWC 1 | ACT 1 | 232 SF |
| 306 | OFFICE | Wood | Carpet 1 | VWC 1 | ACT 1 | 229 SF |
| 307 | OFFICE | Wood | Carpet 1 | VWC 1 | ACT 1 | 125 SF |
| 308 | MECH / ELEC RM | | | | | 98 SF |
| 309 | WOMENS | | | | | 161 SF |
| 310 | MEN | | | | | 161 SF |
| 311 | MISC. /   STORAGE | | | | | 125 SF |
| 312 | OFFICE | Wood | Carpet 1 | VWC 1 | ACT 1 | 229 SF |
| 313 | OFFICE | Wood | Carpet 1 | VWC 1 | ACT 1 | 232 SF |
| 314 | OPEN OFFICE | | | | | 1896 SF |
| 315 | OFFICE | Wood | Carpet 1 | VWC 1 | ACT 1 | 232 SF |
| 316 | OFFICE | Wood | Carpet 1 | VWC 1 | ACT 1 | 229 SF |
| # 1 | STAIR | | | | | 168 SF |

**Figure 10-26** Partial Room Sched. with new data

## Setting up a color-coded floor plan:

With the Room Tags in place you can quickly set up color-coded floor plans. These are plans that indicate (with color) which rooms are Offices, Circulation, Public, etc., based the room name in our example.

18. Switch to **Level 3** view.

19. From the *Drafting* tab select **Color Fill**.  Color Fill

20. Click just below the plan on the right side.

21. Click **OK** to the warning prompt. (Figure 10-27)

**Figure 10-27** Color fill warning

No colors defined

**Figure 10-28** Initial symbol

You will now have a symbol in the view that states: **No colors defined**. (Figure 10-28) You will define the colors next.

22. Select the symbol shown in **Figure 10-28**.

23. Click **Edit Color Scheme...** on the *Options Bar*. (Figure 10-29)

**Figure 10-29** Options Bar – Color Fill key selected

24. Set the **Color By** option to **Name**. This will color the rooms based on the <u>different</u> room names. (Figure 10-30)

Each unique room name will get a different color. Before you finish you will change one *Color* and one *Fill Pattern*.

25. Click on the *Color* for the **Atrium**.

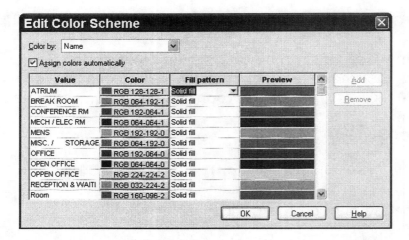

**Figure 10-30** Edit Color Scheme dialog

26. Click the **PANTONE...** button to select a standard Pantone color. (Figure 10-31)

27. Type **365** in the *Find Color* area and press enter. (Figure 10-32)

28. Click **OK** to accept.

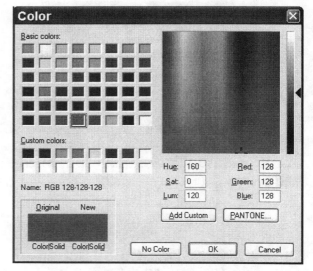

**Figure 10-31** Color selector

29. Now click on the *Fill Pattern* for the **MECH / ELEC RM**.

30. Click the down-arrow & select **Vertical-small** from the list.

31. Click **OK**.

Your plan should look similar to Figure 10-33. The color selected for the Open Office area is too dark; you should adjust it so the room name and number are legible. The last thing you will do is create a toggle between the colored plan and a non-colored plan.

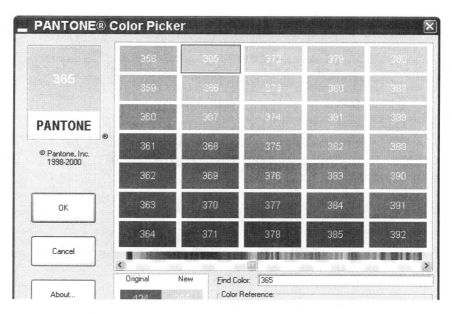

**Figure 10-32** PANTONE Color selector

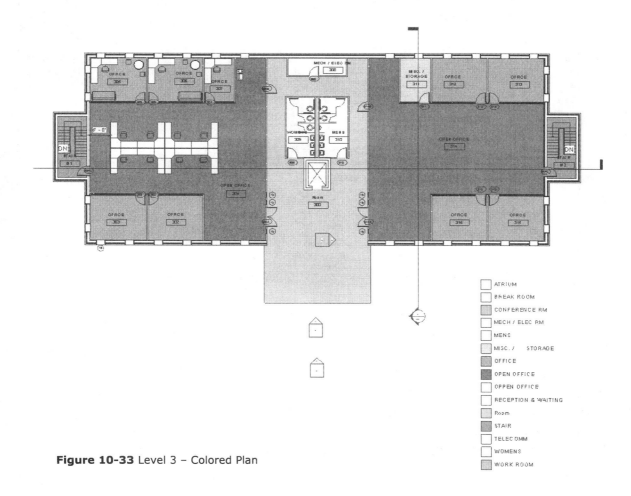

**Figure 10-33** Level 3 – Colored Plan

32. Select the **Color Fill Legend** (inserted just below the plan).

33. Click on the **Properties** button and then click **Edit/New**.

34. Click **Duplicate** and type **No Color**.

35. Click on the **Edit** button (next to the Color Scheme parameter) and set the *Color By* option to **Department**. *FYI: because you do not have department specified, Revit will not assign colors.*

36. Click **OK** to finish back to the plan.

The plan will not have color at this time. Follow these steps to toggle between the color and non-color settings:

37. Select the **Color Fill Legend**.

38. Select the **Color Scheme** you want from the *Type Selector* on the *Options Bar*. (Figure 10-34)

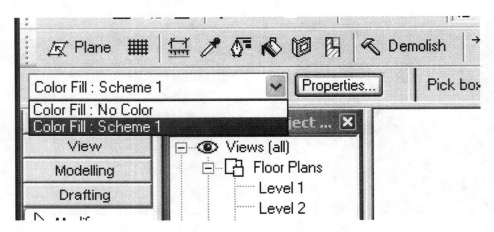

**Figure 10-34** Color scheme type selector

39. **Save** your project as **ex10-4.rvt**.

## Self-Exam:

The following questions can be used as a way to check your knowledge of this lesson. The answers can be found on the last page of this section.

1.   Revit uses the Sweets module to generate Preliminary Estimates. (T/F)

2.   The area for a room is calculated when a room tag is placed. (T/F)

3.   Revit can tag all the doors not currently tagged on a given level with the "tag all not tagged" tool. (T/F)

4.   You can add or remove various fields in a door or room schedule. (T/F)

5.   Use the _____ _____ tool to add color to the rooms in a plan view.

## Review Questions:

The following questions may be assigned by your instructor as a way to assess your knowledge of this section. Your instructor has the answers to the review questions.

1.   You can add a door tag with a leader. (T/F)

2.   You can export your cost report to an HTML file for viewing on the internet. (T/F)

3.   A door can be deleted from the door schedule. (T/F)

4.   The schedule formatting only shows up when you place the schedule on a plot sheet. (T/F)

5.   It is not possible to add the finish information (i.e., base finish, wall finish) to multiple rooms at one time. (T/F)

6.   When setting up a color scheme, you can adjust the color and the

      _____ pattern in the Edit Color Scheme dialog.

7.   Use the _____ dialog to adjust the various fields associated with each room tag in a plan view.

8.   Most door schedules are sorted by the _____ field.

9.   You specify the _____ _____ to allow Revit and RS Means to adjust the cost report to match your area.

10.  Revit provides access to the industry standard _____ color library.

**Notes:**

# Lesson 11
# Office Building: Photo-Realistic Rendering::

You will take a look at Revit's photo-realistic rendering abilities. Rather than reinventing the wheel, Revit chose to use an established architectural rendering program called Accurender (similar to the RS Means for estimating).

## Exercise 11-1:
## Creating an exterior rendering

The first thing you will do is set up a view. You will use the camera tool to do this. This becomes a saved view that can be opened at any time from the Project Browser.

## Creating a Camera view:

1. Open the **Level 1** view and **Zoom All to Fit**, so you can see the entire plan.

2. From the *View* tab, select **Camera**.  Camera

3. Click the mouse in the lower right corner of the screen to indicate the camera eye location. *Notice, before you click, Revit tells you it wants the eye location first on the status bar*.

4. Next click near the atrium curtainwall; see Figure 11-1.

Revit will automatically open a view window for the new camera. Take a minute to look at the view and make a mental note of what you see and don't see in the view (Figure 11-2).

5. Switch back to the **Level 1** plan view.

6. Adjust the camera, using its grips, to look similar to Figure 11-3. *TIP: if the camera is not visible in plan view, right click on the 3D view name in the Project Browser (3D View 1) and select Show Camera.*

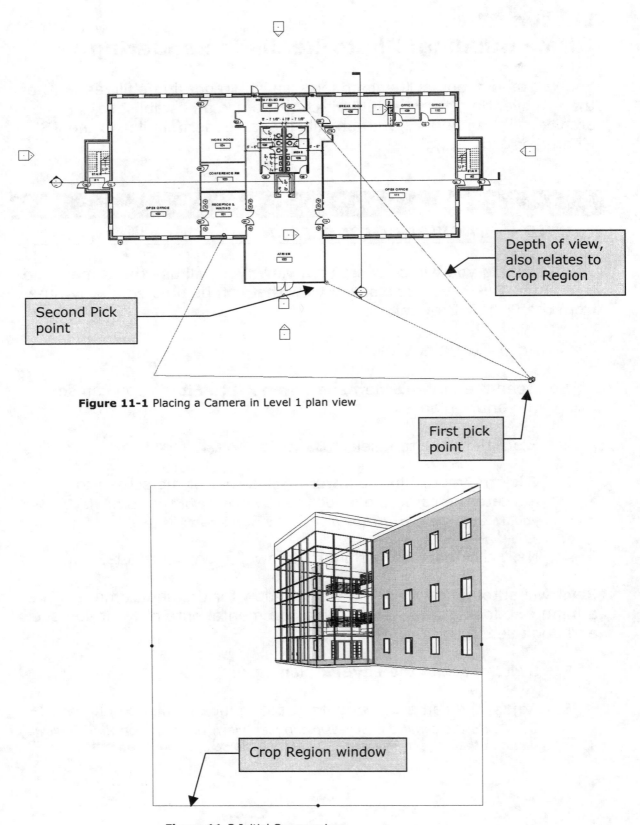

Depth of view, also relates to Crop Region

Second Pick point

**Figure 11-1** Placing a Camera in Level 1 plan view

First pick point

Crop Region window

**Figure 11-2** Initial Camera view

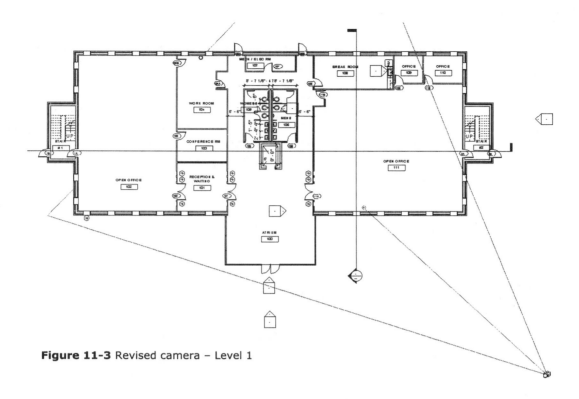

**Figure 11-3** Revised camera – Level 1

7.  Now switch to 3D View 1 and adjust the **Crop Region** to look similar to **Figure 11-4**.

This will be the view we render later in this exercise.

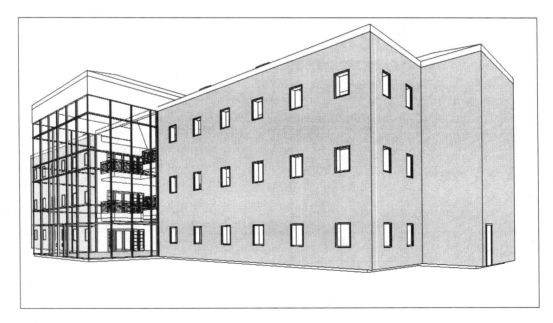

**Figure 11-4** Revised camera – 3d View 1

## Assigning materials to objects:

Materials are scanned images or computer generated representations of the materials your building will be made of.

Typically materials are added while the project is being modeled. For example, when you create a material (using the Materials... command under the Settings menu), you can assign an Accurender material at that time. Of course, you can go back and add or change it later. Next you will change the material assigned for the exterior brick wall.

8.   Switch to **Level 1** plan view.

9.   Select an exterior wall somewhere in plan view.

10.  Click **Properties** from the *Options Bar*.

11.  Click **Edit/New** and then click **Edit** *structure*.

12.  Notice the material selected for the exterior finish is **Masonry – Brick**. (Figure 11-5)

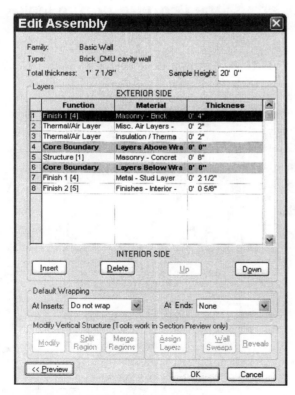

13.  Click **Cancel** three times to close the open dialog boxes.

Now you will take a look that the definition of the material Masonry – Brick.

14.  From the *Settings* menu select **Materials...**

15.  From the Name drop-down list select **Masonry – Brick**. (Figure 11-6)

**Figure 11-5** Exterior wall assembly

16. In the Accurender area, click on the **Select...** button.

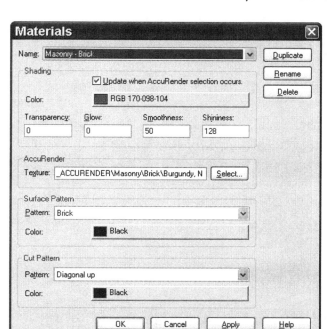

**Figure 11-6** Materials dialog

You will now see Accurender's Material Library dialog. The current material will be selected and displayed. (Figure 11-7)

You can browse through the folders on the left and select any material in the Name list to be assigned to the Masonry – Brick material in Revit. The material does not have to be brick but would be confusing if something else where assigned to the Masonry – Brick material.

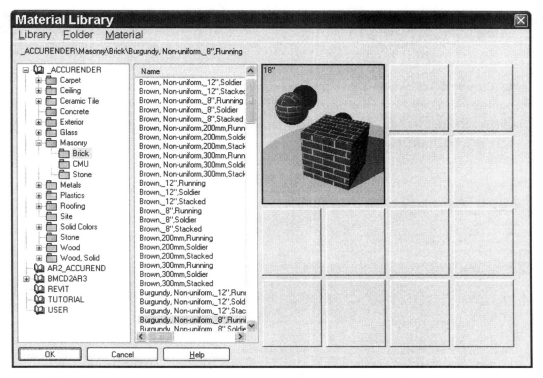

**Figure 11-7** Accurender's Material Library dialog

17. Scroll down in Brick category and select **Yellow,_8",Running**, and then click **OK**.

Notice the Texture listed in the Accurender area is now updated.

18. Click **OK** to close the *Materials* dialog.

Now, when you render, any object (wall, ceiling, etc.) that has the material Masonry – Brick associated with it, will have the Yellow brick on them.

If you need more than one brick color, you simply create a new material in the Material dialog and assign that material to another wall type.

## Setting up the Environment:

You have several options for setting up the building's environment. You can adjust the sun settings, ground plane and sky, to name a few. You will review these options next.

19. Switch to your camera view: **3D View 1**.

20. Select the **Rendering** tab. *TIP: most of the tools are grayed-out if you are not in a 3D view.*

21. Click on the **Settings** tool. (Figure 11-8)

22. Click **Exterior Scene** at the bottom and select **OK** to continue. (Figure 11-9)

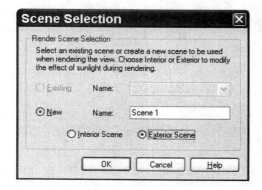

**Figure 11-9** Scene Selection dialog

**Figure 11-8**
Rendering Tab

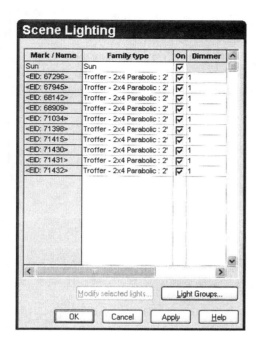

**Figure 11-10** Scene Lighting dialog

23. Click on the Lighting button.

You will now see a dialog similar to the one shown to the left (Figure 11-10).

You will see a Sun and several 2x4 light fixtures. The light fixtures relate to the fixtures you inserted in the reflected ceiling plans. It is very convenient that you can place lights in the ceiling plan and have them ready to render whenever you need to.

24. Click **Cancel**.

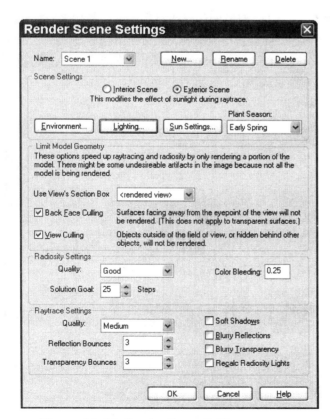

**Figure 11-11** Render Scene Settings

25. Click on **Sun Settings**.

26. On the *Date and Time* tab set (Figure 11-12):
    a. Month: **6**
    b. Day: **30**
    c. Time: **3:00pm**

27. On the *Place* tab set (Figure 11-12):
    a. Maps: *your area*
    b. Pick *your city from the list or click your location on the map*.

28. On the *Settings* tab set the cloudiness to **0.20**. (Figure 11-12)

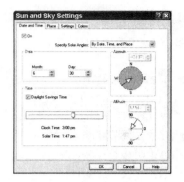  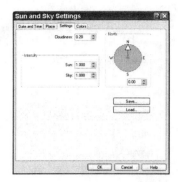

**Figure 11-12**  Accuredner's Sun settings dialog (3 images)

29. Click on the **Environment** button.

30. Check the **Ground Plane** option.

31. When the *Ground Plane* tab opens, click on the **Materials** button.

32. In the *Site* folder, select **Grass, Rye, Dark** and then click **OK** two times to close the dialog boxes.

33. Back in the *Render* Scene Settings dialog, make sure **Exterior Scene** is selected and adjust the **Raytrace Quality** to *Good*.

34. Click **OK**.

Next you will place a few trees into your rendering. You will adjust their exact location so they are near the edge of the framed rendering, so as not to cover too much of the building.

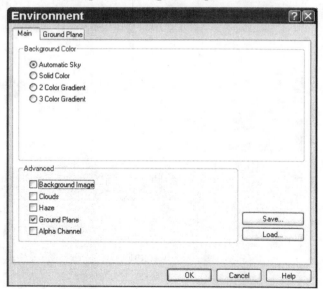

**Figure 11-13**  Accurender's Environment dialog

35. Switch to level 1 plan view and select **Component** from the *Design Bar*.

36. Pick **Tree – Deciduous : Salix Aba 27'** from the *Type Selector* on the *Design Bar*. *FYI, if the tree is not listed in the type selector, click Load from Library and load the Deciduous tree family from the Plantings folder.*

37. Place three trees as shown in **Figure 11-14** (you will make one smaller in a moment).

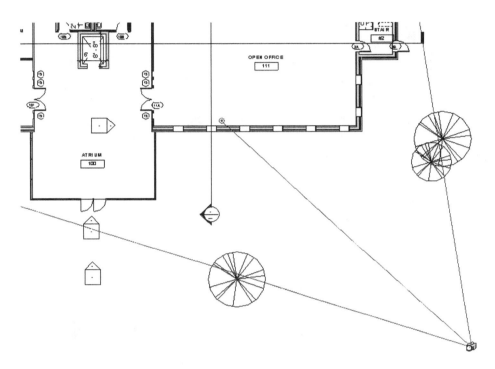

**Figure 11-14** Level 1 with trees added

38. Adjust the trees in plan view, reviewing the effects in the 3D View 1 view, so your 3D view is similar to Figure 11-15.

39. In the level 1 plan view, select the tree that is shown smaller in **Figure 11-14**.

40. Select Properties on the *Option Bar*, and then click *Edit/New*. Click **Duplicate** and enter the name: **Deciduous : Salix Aba 19'**.

41. Click **OK** to close the open dialog boxes.

The previous three steps allow you to have a little more variety in the trees being placed. Otherwise, they would all be the same height, which is not very natural.

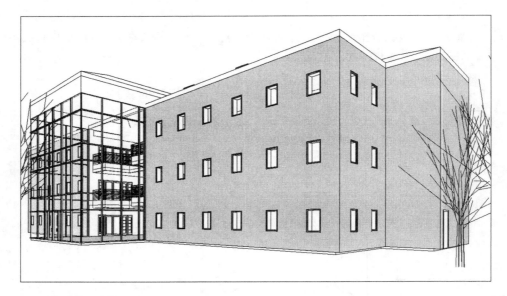

**Figure 11-15**  3D View 1 – with trees

42. Open the **3D View 1** camera view.

43. Click on the **Image Size** button. (Figure 11-8)

44. Change the DPI from 72 to **150**. (Figure 11-16)

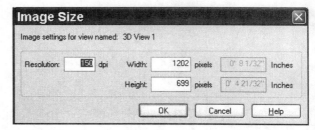

45. Click **Raytrace...** from the Rendering Tab. (Figure 11-8)

**Figure 11-16**  Image Size

46. Click **NO** to the warning about lights being on. (Figure 11-17)

**Figure 11-17**  Lighting warning

You should now have a rendered image similar to Figure 11-18 below. You can increase the quality of the image by adjusting the quality setting in the Settings dialog and by increasing the DPI resolution in the Image Size dialog. However, these higher setting require substantially more time to generate the rendering. The last step before saving the Revit project file is to save the rendered image to a file. *FYI, each time you make changes to the model (that are visible from that view), you will have to re-render the view to gat an updated image.*

**Figure 11-18** Rendered view

47. From the *Render* tab select **Export Image**.

48. Select a *location* and provide a *file name*.

49. Set the Save as type: to **JPEG**.

50. Click **Save**.

The image file you just saved can now be inserted into MS Word or Adobe Photoshop for editing.

51. Save your project as **ex11-1.rvt**.

## Exercise 11-2:
## Rendering an isometric in section

This exercise will introduce you to a view tool called Section Box. This tool is not necessarily related to renderings, but the two tools together can produce some interesting results.

### Setting up the 3D view:

1.  Open file ex11-1.rvt and **Save As ex11-2.rvt**.

2.  Switch to the **Default 3D** view *(not the 3D View 1 from exercise 11-1)*.

3.  *Right-click* in the drawing area and select **View Properties**.

4.  Activate the **Section Box** parameter and then click **OK**.

You should see a box appear around your building, similar to Figure 11-19. When selected, you can adjust the size of the box with it's grips. Anything outside the box is not visible. This is a great way to study a particular area of your building while in an isometric view. You will experiment with this feature next.

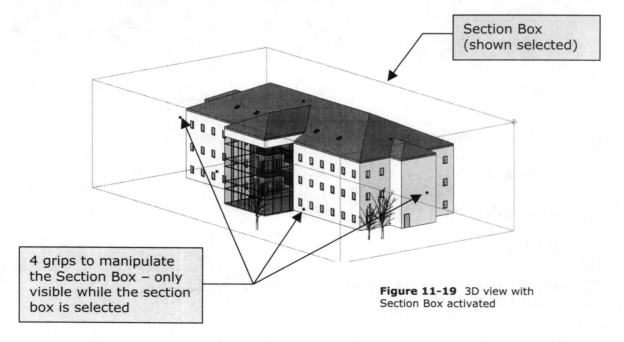

Section Box (shown selected)

4 grips to manipulate the Section Box – only visible while the section box is selected

**Figure 11-19**  3D view with Section Box activated

5.  To practice using the **Section Box**, drag the grips around until your view looks similar to **Figure 11-20**. *TIP: this will require the Dynamically Modify View tool as well.*

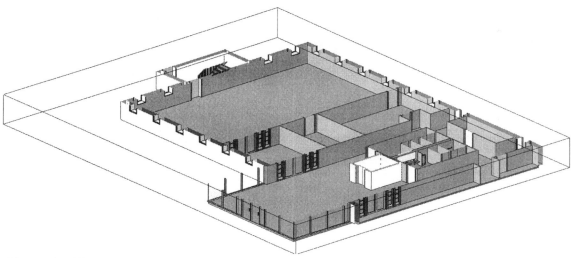

**Figure 11-20**  3D view with adjusted Section Box

This creates a very interesting view of the Level 1 – West Wing. What client would have trouble understanding this drawing?

6.  Now re-adjust the **Section Box** to look similar to **Figure 11-21**.

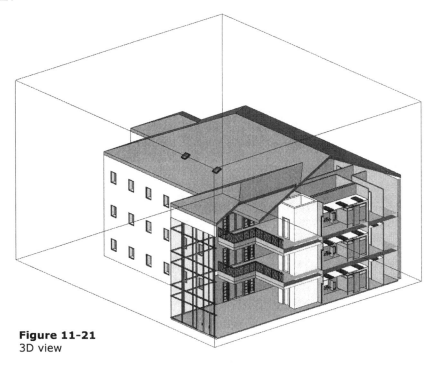

**Figure 11-21**
3D view

7.  From the *Rendering* tab, select **Settings** and change the following (Figure 11-22):
    a. Month: **2** (February)
    b. Day: **28**
    c. Time: **8:30am**

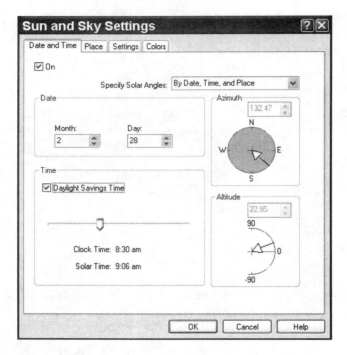

**Figure 11-22**  Modified Sun settings

8.  Select **Raytrace**. You will get a warning stating the rending will take long if the *Region Raytrace* is not used. Click **Cancel**.

9.  Select **Region Raytrace** and select a window around the entire building. *TIP: This tool is nice for checking a material before rendering the entire building, which takes longer.*

The image will take a few minutes to render (depending on the speed of your computer). When finished it should look similar to **Figure 11-23**. Notice that, if an object does not have a material associated with it, the object is rendered using the "shade mode" color.

Both the "shade mode" and "rendered" views have their pluses and minuses. The "shade mode" has nice crisp lines defining all the edges, and a "rendered" image had shadows from the Sun.

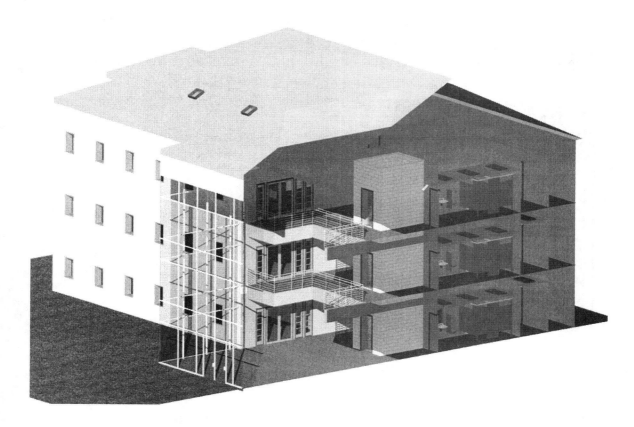

**Figure 11-23** Rendered isometric view

## Adjusting an object's material:

As previously mentioned, most objects already have a material assigned to them. This is great because it allows you to quickly render your project to get some preliminary images. However, they usually need to be adjusted. You will do this next.

10. Switch to **Level 1** plan view and zoom in on the toilet rooms.

11. Select one of the toilet partitions.

12. Click **Properties** from the *Options Bar*.

13. Click the **Edit/Copy**... button.

14. Notice the Toilet Partition parameter is set to **Toilet Partition**. Click this value, then click the down arrow, and then scroll through the list. Notice the list is the defined Materials in this project. Leave this setting as is. (Figure 11-24)

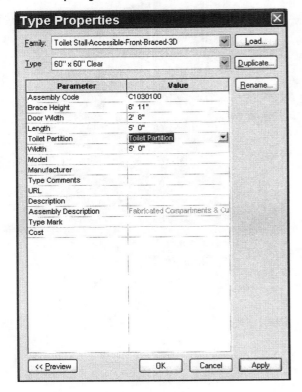

15. **Cancel** the open dialog boxes.

16. Open the Materials dialog from the Settings menu.

17. Select **Toilet Partition** from the *Name* drop-down.

18. Change the Accurender material to: **\Stone \Granite, Black, Polish**. (Figure 11-24)

19. Click **OK** to close the open dialog boxes.

**Figure 11-24** Toilet Partition properties

20. You can now re-render the 3D view and see the results.

21. **Save** your project as ex **11-2.rvt**.

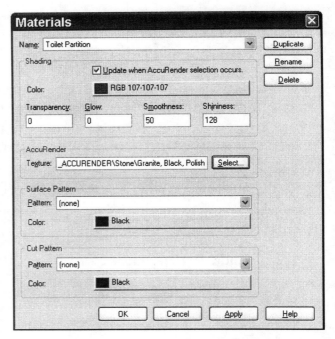

**Figure 11-24** Accurender material selector

## Exercise 11-3:
## Creating an interior rendering

Creating an interior rendering is very similar to an exterior rendering. This exercise will walk through the steps involved in defining exterior light sources and using radiosity to create high quality interior renderings.

### Setting up the camera view:

1.   Open ex11-2.rvt and **Save As ex11-3.rvt**.

2.   Open **Level 2** view.

3.   From the *View* tab, select **Camera**.

4.   Place the *Camera* as shown in **Figure 11-25**.

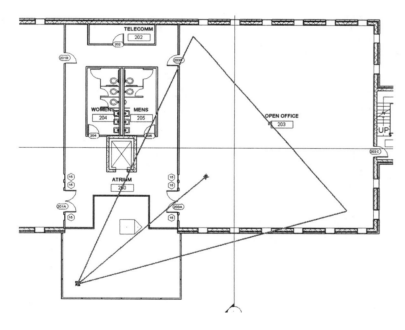

**Figure 11-25**  Camera placed – Level 2 view

Revit uses default heights for the camera and the target. These heights are based on the current level's floor elevation. These reference points can be edited via the camera properties.

Revit will automatically open the newly generated camera view. Your view should look similar to **Figure 11-26**. *FYI, make sure you created the camera on Level 2.*

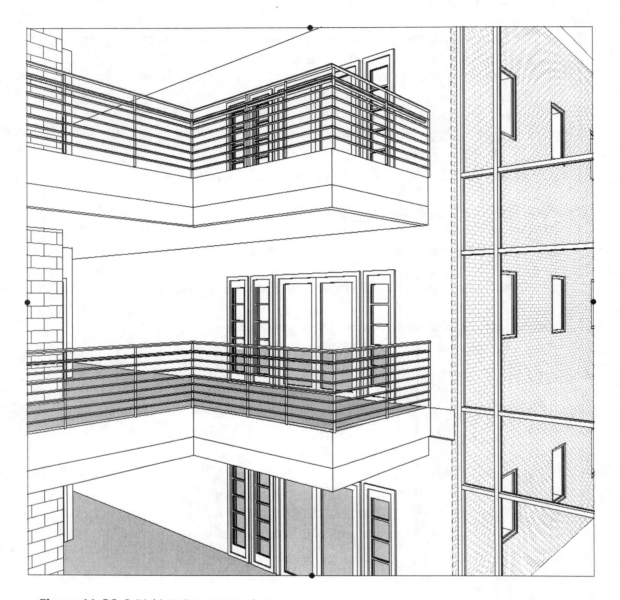

**Figure 11-26** Initial interior camera view

5.  Using the **Crop Region** rectangle, modify the view to look like **Figure 11-27**. *TIP: you will have to switch to plan view to adjust the camera's depth of view to see the trees. Reminder: if the camera does not show in plan view, right-click on the camera view label in the project browser and select Show Camera.*

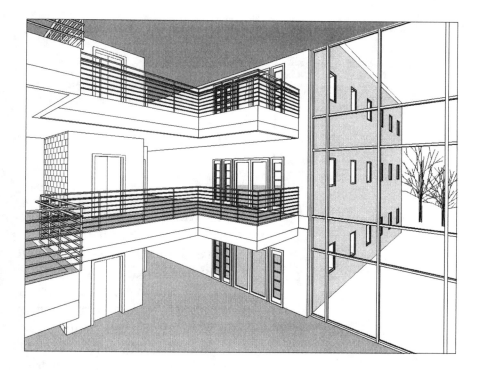

**Figure 11-27**  Modified interior camera

6. Switch back to **Level 2** to see the revised *Camera* view settings.

Notice the field of view triangle is wider based on the changes to the Crop Region. (Figure 11-28)

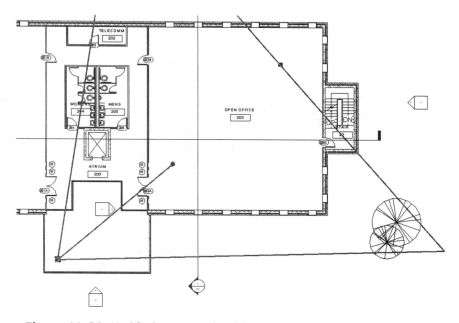

**Figure 11-28**  Modified camera – level 2

7. Select the Camera and click the **Properties** button on the Option Tab. (Figure 11-29)

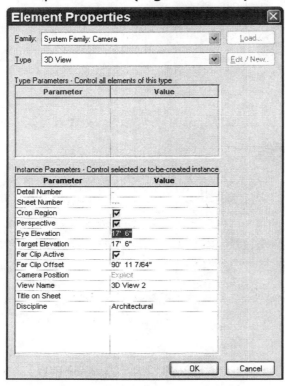

8. Change the **Eye Elevation** to **5'-6"**.

9. Click **OK.**

Your interior camera view should now look similar to **Figure 11-30**. This would be a person standing on level 1 looking up. The vertical lines are distorted due to the wide field of view (crop region). This is similar to what a camera with a 10-15mm lens would get in the finished building.

**Figure 11-29** Camera properties

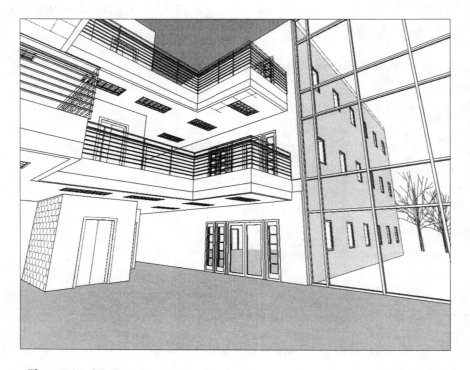

**Figure 11-30** Interior camera view

## Setting up day lighting for radiosity:

Radiosity is a method of calculating natural light for an interior surface. You need to define the exterior light source. Revit (via Accurender) then calculates how the light bounces off different surfaces. This creates a very realistic interior rendering.

10. Switch to the **Default 3D** view.

11. From the *Rendering* tab, select **Daylights...**

12. Select each of the glazing areas (cells) between the curtainwall mullions. When one cell is selected it is shown red while in the *Daylights* tool. You need to select near the perimeter of the cell to select it. Adjust the view to select all the cells on three sides. When finished, all the glass will have a red tint.

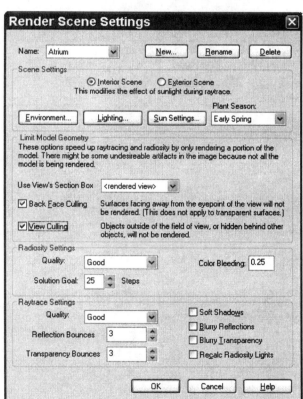

13. Click the **Modify** button to exit the *Daylights* tool.

Next you will adjust the view Setting for Rendering.

14. Click **Settings** from the *Rendering* tab.

15. Click New to create a scene named Atrium.

16. Select Interior Scene. (Figure 11-31)

Next you will run the *Radiosity* tool to calculate the lighting before the *Raytrace* tool is used.

**Figure 11-31** Settings

17. Switch to your interior camera view.

18. Select **Radiate...** from the Rendering tab.

Click **OK** to continue. (Figure 11-32)

Revit will take a few minutes to Radiate the current view. When finished, your view should look similar to **Figure 11-33**.

**Figure 11-32** Warning

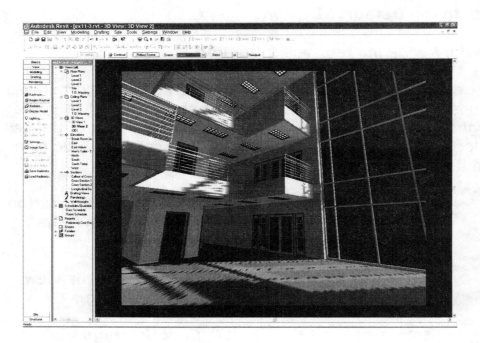

**Figure 11-33** Radiosity

Next you will render the view.

19. Select **Raytrace...** from the *Rendering* tab.

This will take several minutes depending on the speed of your computer. When finished, the view should look similar to **Figure 11-34**.

20. Click **Export Image** from the Rendering tab to save the image to a file on your hard drive. Name the file **Interior Atrium.jpg** (jpeg file format).

**Figure 11-34** Rendered view

You can now open the *Interior Atrium.jpg* file in Adobe Photoshop or similar program to manipulate or print.

> FYI: The rendered image above has ceilings and lights added to each floor in the Atrium that were not added by any previous lesson, unless your in instructor assigned that task as extra work for Lesson 6. You should quickly add this information prior to rendering the view. This will make the rendering look much better.

To toggle back to the normal hidden view, **Display Model** from the *Rendering* tab.

## Rendering a night scene:

One more variation we will look at is rendering the interior atrium view at nighttime. This involves adjusting the sun settings so the Sun is below the horizon and making sure you have the correct number of light fixtures to light the space being rendered.

21. Click **Settings** on the *Rendering* tab.

22. Click **New** at the top to create a new *Scene*.

23. Type **Atrium Night** for the *Scene* name.

24. Click on **Sun Setting** and adjust the *Time* to **4:00am**.

25. Click **OK** to save and close the open dialog boxes.

26. While in the camera view for the Atrium, click on the **Radiate...** button.

27. On the *Options Bar*, change the Scene selector to **Atrium Night**.

The view will be reset and ready to run the Radiate tool again. This is necessary because the exterior lighting is different and would affect the interior lighting solution. *FYI, you would also need to rerun Radiate if you change anything in the Atrium area of the model*.

28. Select **Radiate...** from the *Rendering* tab.

29. When *Radiate* is finished, Click **Raytrace**.

When Raytrace is completed you will have a night view of your interior atrium. This clearly shows the effect the 2x4 light fixtures have on the rendering, as they are the primary light source for this rendering. Your image should look similar to **Figure 11-35**.

You can also try this (especially if you have placed light fixtures for the entire building) on your exterior camera view. Nighttime renderings can be very dramatic.

**Figure 11-35** Rendered nighttime view

Notice you can see reflections in the curtainwall glass. Revit accurately renders reflective surfaces like glass and shiney or polished metal (like the elevator doors). This creates a more realistic rendering.

30. **Save** your project as **11-3.rvt**.

## Exercise 11-4:
## Adding people to the rendering

Revit provides a few RPC people to add to your renderings. These are files from a popular company that provides 3D photo content for use in renderings (http://www.archvision.com). You can buy this content in groupings (like college students) or per item. In addition to people, they offer items like cars, plants, trees, office equipment, etc.

### Text

1. Open ex11-3.rvt and **Save As 11-4.rvt**.

2. Switch to **Level 2** view.

3. Select the **Component** tool from the *Rendering* tab.

4. Click the **Load from Library** button on the *Options Bar*.

5. Browse to the **Entourage** folder and select both the **RPC Male** and **RPC Female** files (using the Ctrl key to select both at once) and click load.

6. Place one **Male** and one **Female** as shown in **Figure 11-36**.

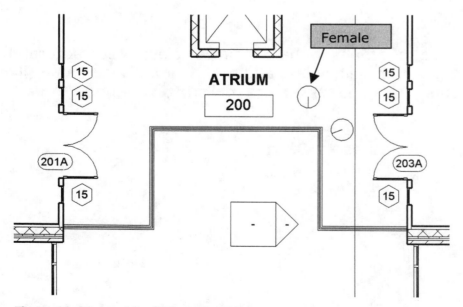

**Figure 11-36** Level 2 – RPC people added

The line in the circle (Figure 11-36) represents the direction a person is looking. You simply Rotate the object to make adjustments.

7.   Switch to **Level 1** view.

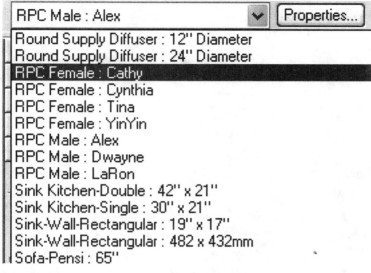

**Figure 11-37** Type Selector – Options Bars

8.   Place a few of the other people available (similar to Figure 11-38)

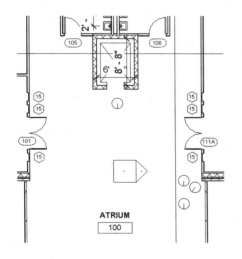

9.   Switch to your interior atrium camera view.

10.  Select **Settings** on the *Rendering* tab.

11.  Set the *Scene* to **Atrium**.

12.  Click **OK**.

13.  Click **Raytace** to render the view with the people in the view.

**Figure 11-38** Level 1 – people added

Your rendering should now have people in it and look similar to **Figure 11-39**.

**Figure 11-39** Interior Atrium view with people added

Adding people and other "props" gives your model a sense of scale and makes it look a little more realistic. After all, architecture is for people. These objects can be viewed from any angle. Try a new camera view from a different angle to see how the people adjust to match the view and perspective.

14. **Save** your project as **ex11-4.rvt**.

FYI: As with other families and components, the more you add to your project, the bigger your project file becomes. It is a good idea to load only the items you need and delete the unused items via the Project Browser.

## Self-Exam:

The following questions can be used as a way to check your knowledge of this lesson. The answers can be found on the last page of this section.

1. Creating a camera adds a view to the Project Browser list. (T/F)

2. Accurender materials are defined in Revit's Materials dialog box. (T/F)

3. After inserting a light fixture, you need to adjust several setting before rendering in Accurender and getting light from the fixture. (T/F)

4. You can adjust the season, which affects how the trees are rendered. (T/F)

5. Use the _____ _____ tool to remove a large portion of the model.

## Review Questions:

The following questions may be assigned by your instructor as a way to assess your knowledge of this section. Your instructor has the answers to the review questions.

1. You cannot pick a material for the ground plane. (T/F)

2. Radiosity is best used on exterior scenes. (T/F)

3. Adding components and families to your project does not make the project file bigger. (T/F)

4. Using the Radiosity feature adds a significant amount of time to the rending process. (T/F)

5. The RPC people can only be viewed from one angle. (T/F)

6. You have to use the _____ tool (to define the exterior light source) before using the Radiate tool.

7. Adjust the _____ _____ to make more of a perspective view visible.

8. You use the _____ tool to load & insert RPC people.

9. You can adjust the Eye Elevation of the camera via the camera's

_____.

10. What is the file size of (completed) exercise 11-4? _____ MB

**Notes:**

# Lesson 12
# Office Building: Construction Documents Set::

This lesson will look at bringing everything you have drawn thus far together onto sheets. The sheets, once set up, are ready for plotting. Basically, you place the various views you have created on sheets. The scale for each view is based on the scale you set while drawing that view (which is important to have set correctly because it affects the text and symbol sizes. When finished setting up the sheets, you will have a set of drawings ready to print, individually or all at once.

## *Exercise 12-1:*
## *Setting up a sheet*

Creating a Sheet view:

1. Open ex11-4.rvt and Save As 12-1.rvt.

2. Select **Sheet...** from the *View* tab.    📑 Sheet...

Next Revit will prompt you for a Titleblock to use. The template file you started with only has one; that's the one you will use. (Figure 12-1)

3. Click OK to select the **E1 30x42 Horizontal** titleblock.

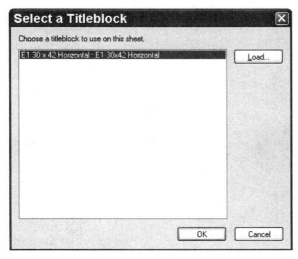

> **Notice** a new view shows up in the Project Browser under the heading: Sheets. Once you get an entire CD set ready, this list can be very long.

**Figure 12-1** Select a Titleblock

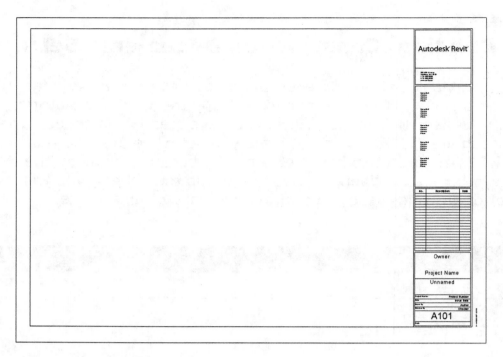

**Figure 12-2** Initial Titleblock view

4. **Zoom** into the sheet number area (lower right corner).

5. Adjust the text to look similar to **Figure 12-3**.

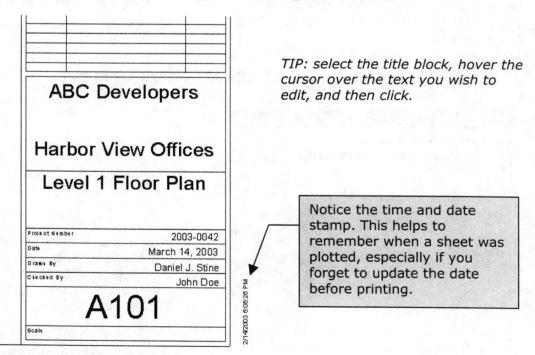

*TIP: select the title block, hover the cursor over the text you wish to edit, and then click.*

Notice the time and date stamp. This helps to remember when a sheet was plotted, especially if you forget to update the date before printing.

**Figure 12-3** Revised Titleblock data

6. **Zoom out** so you can see the entire sheet.

7. With the sheet fully visible, click and drag the **Level 1** label (under floor plans) from the *Project Browser* onto the sheet view.

You will see a red box that represents the extents of the view you are placing on the current sheet.

8. Move the cursor around until the box is somewhat centered on the sheet (this can be adjusted later at any time).

Your view should look similar to **Figure 12-4**.

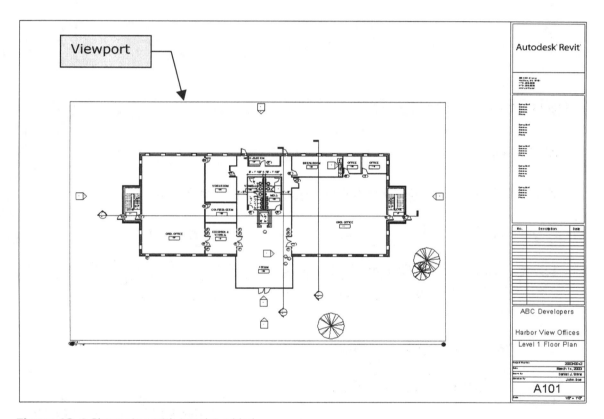

**Figure 12-4** Sheet view with Level 1 added

9. Click the mouse in a "white" area (not on any lines) to deselect the Level 1 drawing. Notice the red box goes away.

10. **Zoom In** on the lower left corner to view the drawing identification symbol that Revit automatically added. (Figure 12-5)

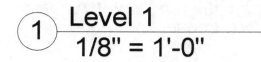

**Figure 12-5** Drawing ID tag

Notice:
The drawing number for this sheet is added. The next drawing you add will be number 2.

The view name is listed. This is another reason to rename the elevation and section views as you create them.

Also notice that the drawing scale is listed. Again, this comes from the scale setting for the level 1 view.

11. **Zoom Out** to see entire sheet again.

12. Add two more sheets and set up Levels 2 and 3 on them:
    a. Sheet A102  →  Level 2 Floor Plan
    b. Sheet A103  →  Level 3 Floor Plan

> **Notice** when you create a new sheet, most of the titleblock is filled in and the number has increased by 1. This pre-entered info can be changed if needed.

## Setting up the Exterior Elevations:

Next you will set up the exterior elevations on the A200 series sheets.

13. Create a new Sheet and adjust the title block data:
    a. Sheet Title:        Exterior Elevations
    b. Sheet Number:    A200

14. Drag the South elevation view onto the sheet. Place the drawing near the lower right.

15. Drag the North elevation view onto the sheet. Place the drawing so that the drawing title tag is aligned (Revit will snap to this position vertically).

Your drawing should look similar to Figure 12-6.

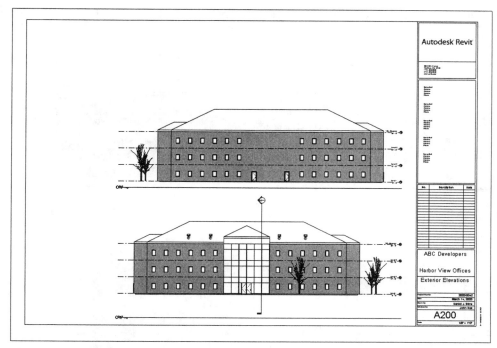

**Figure 12-6** North & South exterior elevations

Next you will turn off the trees in the south view. Normally you would turn them off in all views. However, you will only turn them off in the south view to show that you can control visibility per view on a sheet.

16. Click near the edge of the drawing to select the viewport (reference Figure 12-4).

17. Now **Right-Click** and select **Activate View** from the pop-up menu.

At this point you are in the viewport and can make changes to the project model to control visibility, which is what you will do next.

18. Right-click in the "white space" and select **View Properties...**

19. Click the **Edit** button next to *Visibility*.

20. In the Visibility dialog **Uncheck Planting**.

21. Close the open dialog boxes.

22. Right-click anywhere in the drawing area and select **Deactivate View** from the pop-up menu.

Now the trees are turned off for the South Elevation but not the North.

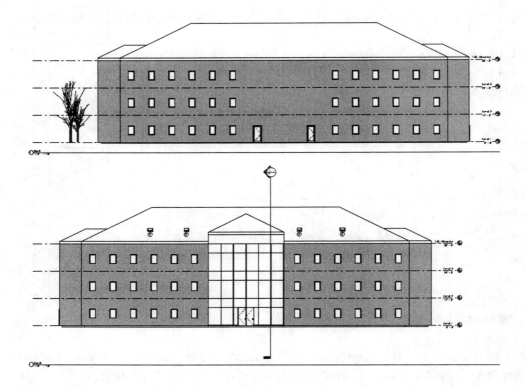

**Figure 12-7** North & South exterior (trees removed from south view)

23. Create another Sheet for the other two exterior elevations (East and West); the sheet should be number **A201**.

Now you will stop for a moment and notice that Revit is automatically referencing the drawings as you place them on sheets.

24. Switch to **Level 1** (see Figure 12-8).

Notice in Figure 12-8 that the number A200 represents the sheet number that the drawing can be found on. The number one (1) is the drawing number to look for on sheet A200.

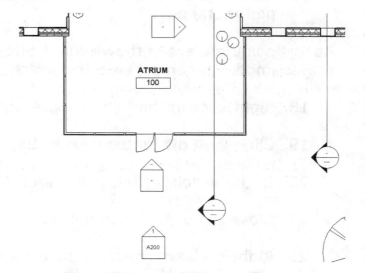

**Figure 12-8** Level 1 – elev. Reference tag filled-in

## Setting up Sections:

25. Create a sheet numbered **A300** and titled **Building Sections**.

26. Add a section, in plan view, through the atrium area.

27. Add the three building sections as shown in **Figure 12-9**.

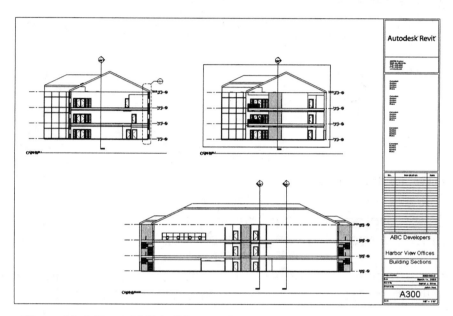

**Figure 12-9** Sheet A300 building sections

28. Switch to Level 1 plan view and zoom into the area shown in Figure 12-10.

Notice, again, that the reference bubbles are automatically filled in when the referenced view is placed on a sheet. If the drawing is moved to another sheet, the reference bubbles are automatically updated.

You can also see in Figure 12-9 (above) that the reference bubbles on the building sections are filled in.

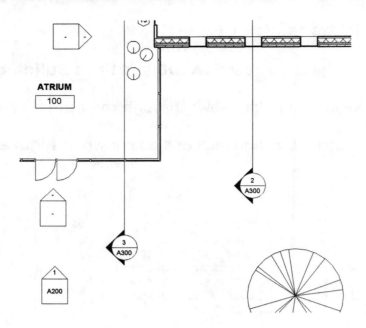

**Figure 12-10** Level 1 – Section ref's filled in

**Question**: on a large project with hundreds of views, how do I know for sure if I have placed every drawing on a sheet?

**Answer**: Revit has a feature, in the Project Browser, that can hide all the views that have been placed on a sheet. You will try this next.

1.  Take a general look at the Project Browser to see how many views are listed. (Figure 12-12)

2.  **Right-Click** on the **Views (all)** label at the top in *Project Browser*, and then select **Hide Views on Sheets**. (Figure 12-11)

3.  Notice the list in the Project Browser is now smaller. (Figure 12-13)

**Figure 12-11** Project Browser

The Project Browser now only shows drawing views that have not been placed onto a sheet. Of course, you could have a few views that do not need to be placed on a sheet, but this feature will help eliminate errors.

Next you will reset the Project Browser.

32. Right-click on **Views (not on sheet)** label at the top in Project Browser and then click **Show All**.

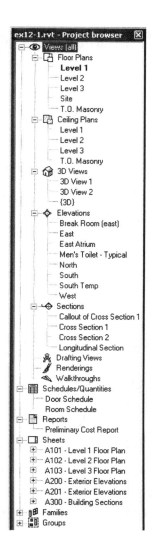

Figure 12-12 Project Browser

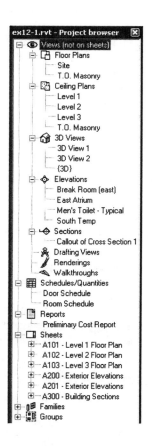

**Figure 12-13** Project Browser (filtered view)

33. **Save** your project as **ex12-1.rvt**.

## *Exercise 12-2:*
## *Printing a set of drawings*

Revit has the ability to print an entire set of drawing, in addition to printing individual sheets. You will study this now.

### Printing a set of drawings

1.  **Open ex12-1.rvt**.

2.  Select **Print** from the *File* pull-down menu.

3.  In the *Print range* area, click the option **Selected views/ sheets**. (Figure 12-14)

4.  Click the **Select...** button within the *Print range* area.

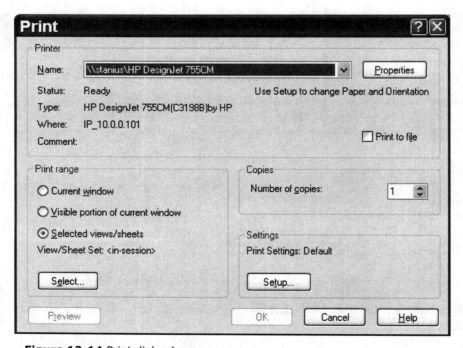

**Figure 12-14** Print dialog box

You should now see a listing of all views and sheets. (Figure 12-15)

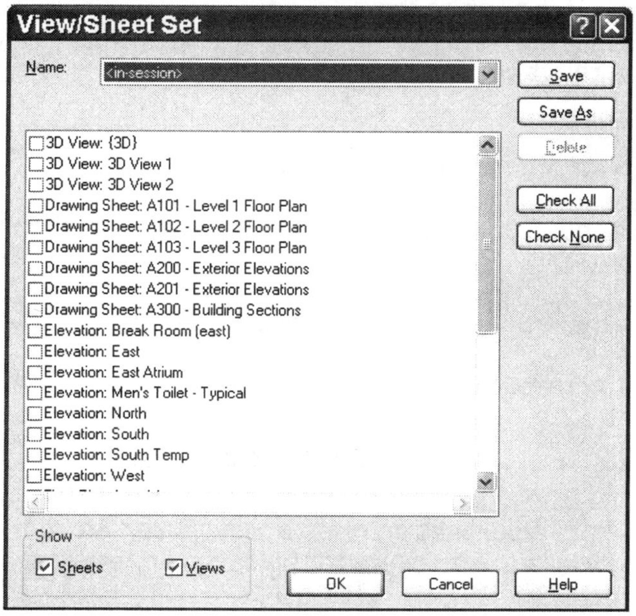

**Figure 12-15** Selecting tool for printing

Notice at the bottom you can Show both Sheets and Views, or each separately. Because you are printing a set of drawing you will want to see only the sheets.

5.  **Uncheck** the **Views** option.

The list is now limited to just sheets set up in your project.

6.  Select all the Drawing Sheets.

---

**FYI:** Once you have selected the sheets to be plotted you can click Save.

This will save the list of selected drawing to a name you choose. Then, the next time you need to print those sheets, you can select the name from the drop-down list at the top (Figure 12-15).

On very large projects (e.g. 20 plan sheets) you could have a Plans list saved, a Laboratory Interior Elevations list saved, Etc.

---

7.  Click **OK** to close the **View/Sheet Set** dialog.

8.  IF YOU ACTUALLY WANT TO PRINT A FULL SET OF DRAWINGS, you can do so now by clicking OK. Otherwise click **Cancel**.

9.  You do not need to save the file at this time.

[End of exercise 12-2]

## Self-Exam:
The following questions can be used as a way to check your knowledge of this lesson. The answers can be found on the last page of this section.

1. You have to manually fill in the reference bubbles after setting up the sheets. (T/F)

2. You cannot control the visibility of objects per viewport. (T/F)

3. It is possible to see a listing of only the views that have not been placed on a sheet via the Project Browser. (T/F)

4. You only have to enter your name on one titleblock, not all. (T/F)

5. Use the _____ tool to create another drawing sheet.


## Review Questions:
The following questions may be assigned by your instructor as a way to assess your knowledge of this section. Your instructor has the answers to the review questions.

1. You need to use a special command to edit text in the titleblock. (T/F)

2. The template you started with has several titleblocks to choose from. (T/F)

3. You only have to enter the project name on one sheet, not all. (T/F)

4. The scale of a drawing placed on a sheet is determined by the scale set in that view's properties. (T/F)

5. You can save a list of drawing sheets to be plotted. (T/F)

6. Use the _____ _____ tool to edit the model from a sheet view.

7. The reference bubbles will not automatically update if a drawing is moved to another sheet. (T/F)

8. On new sheets, the sheet number on the titleblock will increase by one from the previous sheet number. (T/F)

*Self-Exam Answers:*
**1** – F, **2** – F, **3** – T, **4** – F, **5** – Sheet

# Index